A Double Dose of Hard Luck

The Extraordinary True Story of a
Two-Time Prisoner of War
Lt. Col. Charles Lee Harrison

LEO AIME LABRIE
with
THERESA MCLAUGHLIN

PAGE PUBLISHING, INC.
New York, NY

First originally published by Page Publishing, Inc. 2016

ISBN 978-1-68409-211-6 (Paperback)
ISBN 978-1-68409-212-3 (Digital)

Printed in the United States of America

Lt. Col. Charles Lee Harrison, USMC

FOREWORD

I first became acquainted with Charles Harrison at the Marine Corps Recruit Depot at San Diego in July of 1958. At that time, I was a first lieutenant who was newly posted as a series officer in F Company Second Recruit Training Battalion. Charlie was then a captain and serving as one of the inspectors for the commanding general of the recruit training command. Consequently, I would frequently notice Captain Harrison observing our recruit platoons from a discreet distance while they received training from their drill instructors.

I recall that my fellow lieutenants and I grew in awe of the captain when we learned that this soft-spoken, humble, gentlemanly officer who always greeted us with a warm smile was able to claim a wartime experience so extraordinary as to be almost unbelievable. Captain Harrison, we were told, had the unfortunate distinction of being only one of two Marines to have ever suffered captivity as a prisoner of war (POW) twice in two separate conflicts. The first time was during WWII, when he became a prisoner of the Japanese army for forty-five months, following the siege of Wake

Island; the second time was during the Korean War, when he, along with 150 other Marines, became surrounded and were captured by the Chinese communist forces (CCF) at the Chosin Reservoir Campaign on November 29, 1950. He remained in captivity of the CCF until he, along with seventeen fellow POWs, managed to escape from their captors six months later. Needless to say, Captain Harrison never discussed his POW experiences with the likes of us, and of course, we knew better than to raise the subject with him.

In 1994, after I had completed thirty-five years as a serving Marine officer and three additional years as the director of security for the federal aviation administration, my wife, Cathy, and I left Washington, DC, to return to the town and house in which I had been raised in Grass Valley, California. Within a year of returning to my hometown, I was pleasantly surprised to learn that Lieutenant Colonel Charles Harrison had likewise selected Grass Valley as his family home of residence after he had retired from the Marine Corps on June 30, 1969.

Although Charlie and I volunteered our time and energies to different community nonprofits, we nevertheless shared a keen interest in military history and frequently met for lunch to discuss what we were reading or to celebrate the Marine Corps birthday with our wives. Also, in June 1996, Cathy and I were privileged to be included with Charles and Mary's many friends and family members when they celebrated their golden wedding anniversary. Sadly, we were also present at Mary's funeral in late October of 1999 at St. Patrick's Catholic Church and for her internment in the Greenwood Catholic Cemetery.

A few months after the September 11 terrorist attack, I was doing some research at the Marine Corps history division, which was then located at the Washington, DC Navy Yard. One day I happened to mention to Fred Allison, the oral historian for the division, my relationship with retired Lieutenant Colonel Charles Harrison. Fred knew of Colonel Harrison and gave me a transcript of an oral history interview that had been taken from then Staff Sergeant Harrison and several other of his fellow POWs in May of 1951. The interviews were conducted soon after the POWs had escaped their CCF captors and were returned to the custody of US forces in Korea. Fred went on to suggest that I conduct an oral tape interview of Charlie's experiences as a US Marine for the history division at Headquarters Marine Corps. If Colonel Harrison would agree to the interview, Fred said he would provide me with a written interviewer's guide and all the blank tapes that I would need.

When I initially raised the question of an oral interview with Charlie, he was not keen on the idea. Eventually, however, when he considered that perhaps he should do this for his children and grandchildren, he gave me the go-ahead to proceed. In order to prepare myself, I read everything I could find on the Wake Island campaign. Of particular value and the account that I found most useful was *Facing Fearful Odds: The Siege of Wake Island* by Gregory J. W. Urwin. Throughout my interview on the Wake Island phase, I kept this six-hundred-page volume at my side to verify facts, such as dates that Charlie could not quite recall. For example, the August date that Private Harrison, along with the initial group of First Defense Battalion Marines, arrived off Wake Island and began off-loading their equipment from the USS *Regulus* was easily confirmed by Dr. Urwin's book.

The taping schedule that we established was two 1-hour sessions each week for five weeks. Starting with Charles growing up in Oklahoma to his retirement from the Marine Corps in 1969 resulted in a total of ten hours of oral tapes. Throughout the process, Charles's memory of names and events never ceased to amaze me. For instance, he was still able to rattle off the serial number of his .03 Springfield service rifle. This was the same rifle that had been issued to him as a recruit in San Diego in 1939. My, how he must have cherished that rifle.

In describing the circumstances of losing his beloved .03 Springfield, I remember his face grew sad when he told me, "It was customary during the air raids on wake for the three-inch anti-aircraft batteries to continue firing at the Japanese bombers until they released their bombs. Then our gun crew would dive for their holes or underground bunkers." Apparently, on one of the last raids, Charlie's rifle was left leaning outside a bunker when his gun position received almost a direct hit from a bomb. Charlie emerged as the planes departed to find his rifle had been shattered by a large piece of shrapnel. "It was as if I had lost my best friend," he lamented.

Once the interviews were finished, I shipped the tapes off to the history division at Headquarters Marine Corps. Fred Allison was pleased to have them and graciously made extra copies for Charles to pass on to members of his family, along with written transcripts.

I would like to commend Leo LaBrie and Theresa McLaughlin, for their hard work and dedication in preparing this splendid biography of my long-standing friend and fellow Marine. In my view, their account of Charles Lee Harrison's life is a fitting tribute to a remarkable human being. During his thirty-year career as a US Marine, Charles Harrison repeatedly distinguished himself as he fought and bled for his country in three major wars. Moreover, during two of those conflicts, he suffered a total of fifty-one months of extremely harsh and oftentimes brutally dehumanizing treatment while in the hands of our enemies. Yet despite his agonizing years behind barbed wire, Charles Harrison never became bitter, dejected, or spiritually broken. Instead, he continued to fight and resist against the enemy with the only weapons left to him—his faith and his courage.

Orlo K. Steele
Major General (ret.), USMC

ACKNOWLEDGMENTS

Richard Grosse
Lt. Col. Charles Lee Harrison (deceased)
Beverly Harrison
Theresa McLaughlin
Maj. Gen. Orlo K. Steele USMC (retired)
Jane Harrison Williams

Dear Colonel Harrison, as we approach the 60th anniversary of the fall of Wake Island, I want to take a moment to thank you for the lifetime of exemplary service you have given to the nation. You have never been one to seek recognition, but I believe this occasion calls for an exception. Over three decades as a Marine, you distinguished yourself in battle during some of the most pivotal conflicts of the 20th century, to include the Wake Island campaigns in World War II, the Korean War and Vietnam. That alone is worthy of recognition, yet your record of valor and combat extends to circumstances far greater than most have had to endure. The tremendous courage with which you faced more than four years of captivity by the enemy in two separate conflicts is nothing short of extraordinary. Under such conditions, other men might have given up hope, but you did not. Your story of unfailing bravery against insurmountable odds is an inspiration to us all, and although there are many who will never know the tremendous sacrifices you've made in defense of the nation's freedom, the nation is forever in your debt.[1]

—General James L. Jones,
Commandant, US Marine Corps,
December 13, 2001

---

[1]   Letter to Charles Harrison from General James L. Jones, commandant, USMC, December 13, 2001.

GROWING UP

The journey of this extraordinary man who never gave up hope, even under the most extreme conditions, began in the town of Sand Springs, near Tulsa, Oklahoma, on March 21, 1921. That is the day that Charles Lee Harrison was born to Daniel and Adeline. The close-knit Harrison family, which included siblings Robert, Daniel, Elizabeth, Ruth, and Peggy, could not have predicted the dangerous and life-threatening experiences that awaited their son and brother, nor the courageous and valorous manner in which he would deal with those circumstances.

Charles was raised on two acres in the country, with a productive vegetable garden, a Jersey cow which provided milk so rich it was almost pure cream, and a flock of chicken. Dan Harrison never held a high-paying job, and he and his family worked hard to provide for themselves. They knew how to live off the land and were able to make it through even the toughest Depression years with their strong faith and dogged determination.

In the autumn of 1922, when Charles was just one year old, the first Sunday school in the community was organized by a small group of Free Will Methodists and held its meetings in the basement of the home of Charles's parents. Eventually, this Sunday school found a permanent location and grew to become the Bruner Hill Community Church. In 1952, in honor of the contributions made by the Harrisons, the congregation changed the name of the church to the Harrison Memorial Methodist Church, and it still exists under that name today.[2]

From this hardworking, devout, and loving family, Charles grew into a boy who had a strong will and an ability to take care of himself. He and his siblings were all expected to contribute to the family and to the cost of their own education as soon as they were old enough to do so.

At the age of twelve, Charles was hired for a summer job on a forty-acre farm. It was hard work walking in a large cornfield behind an old mule with a five-tooth cultivator from dawn to dark. As the end of that summer approached, he assisted with the baling of hay and felt very grown up when he was allowed to drive a 1926 model Chevrolet flatbed truck to haul the baled hay from the field to the barn. At other times in his youth, Charles also worked as a short-order cook and a clerk in a dime store. He spent part of one summer working for an ice-cream company. He thought it was fun to be dipping ice cream and meeting other kids but always felt that he could and should be more productive.

---

[2]   Dan M. Harrison, *A Brief History of Harrison Memorial United Methodist Church*, 1948.

By the time Charles was in high school, he was in good physical condition. He was interested in high school athletics but did not feel that he was very good at any of them. He tried out for wrestling and football, but during his first week of football, he broke his ankle, which put him on the sidelines for that season, and after that, he simply lost interest. He took on the job of official photographer for his high school newspaper, and he continued to enjoy and excel at the art of photography throughout his life.

The Harrison family lived about three miles from the high school. In order to keep in shape, Charles would jog to school and back along the railroad tracks whenever the weather permitted. This conditioning allowed him to get hired for a summer job as a lifeguard at Sand Springs Lake, a clear freshwater lake with a sandy beach. Charles was paid $10 per week for this job, which was a fairly generous salary for a youth at the time. He was a good-looking young man, and while working at the lake, he had the opportunity to meet a number of attractive girls, which he said, "Meant quite a bit at the time, but I didn't know what to do about it." In addition to the pretty girls, many professional wrestlers toured through Tulsa, and most of them worked out at the lake where Charles was lifeguarding. Many of these wrestlers were former Marines.

In the winter, Charles took up ice skating and formed an ice hockey league. Tulsa had a good ice rink at the old coliseum, where, for twenty-five cents, you could ice-skate to pipe organ music for two hours. Charles had an adolescent crush on Sonja Henie, an ice-skater who was quite famous and popular at the time. He clipped photos and stories about Sonja Henie from newspapers and magazines and created an entire scrapbook devoted to her.[3]

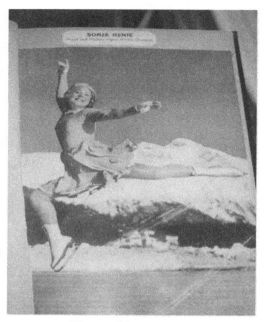

Photo of Sonja Henie
from Charles Harrison's scrapbook

Along with Sonja Henie, Charles was also drawn to a particular young woman at the skating rink. Mary Patricia Hogan was an attractive Irish Catholic girl from Tulsa who attended high school at a convent in Paola, Kansas. Charles and Mary became very attached to each other, as Charles contemplated what he wanted to do with the rest of his life.

Charles spent some time as a chauffeur for a private family, maintaining and driving their car, but he was get-

---

[3]   Interview with Jane Harrison Williams, 2015.

ting tired of the menial jobs he held and knew that he needed to do something that he considered to be more worthwhile. He was fascinated by the former Marines he had met while lifeguarding, which included Danny Savage, Frankie Taylor, LeRoy McGuirk, and Bob Keniston. He remembered their sea stories and felt that this might be the direction he should follow. A high school diploma and parental permission were required for enlistment into the Marine Corps, as Charles was only seventeen years old. After earning his high school diploma on May 17, 1938, he had to convince his parents to allow him to enlist. Charles's mother was reluctant, but his father had been in the Army Quartermaster Corps in World War I and thought the experience would be good for Charles, so both parents eventually agreed to sign his enlistment papers.

At that time, it was not possible to enlist in Oklahoma. A young man was required to get a physical exam at his own expense, and the results of that exam were mailed by the doctor to the Marine Corps Recruiting Office in Dallas, Texas. The initial exam was to make sure that the applicants met the physical requirements. They had to be at least 5'9", with a weight proportionate to their height. They had to have a minimum number of sound opposing teeth and no background of disease or injury that could hinder their recruitment.

After his initial exam, Charles received one piece of mail which said "Show up on the 19th of September and you will be reexamined and determine if you make it." About fourteen young men from Oklahoma, Texas, Arkansas, and

Louisiana received the same letter. All these young men were required to make their own way to Dallas, at their own expense, for the follow-up exam on September 19, 1939. Charles's newly married sister and her husband were heading out on their honeymoon, and Charles was able to ride to Dallas with them.

On September 19, 1939, Charles was deemed qualified to join the Marine Corps. At least four of the other recruits were rejected, so the remaining recruits who qualified were sent to San Diego for basic training, transported on a steam train with open coaches. Thus, Charles Lee Harrison enlisted in the Marine Corps in 1939 at the age of eighteen with the rank of private.

THE WAR YEARS
WWII

Some historians believe that the actual beginning of World War II was on July 7, 1937, when the Marco Polo Bridge incident led to a prolonged war between Japan and China. Most historians, however, date the beginning of WWII to September 1, 1939, when Germany invaded Poland. It was after this event in 1939 that Private Charles Harrison reported to the Marine Corps base in San Diego for his basic training. The cost of his transportation was paid for by the Marine Corps, but it took three days just to get from Dallas, Texas, to Los Angeles. By the time he and his fellow recruits got out of the state of Texas, they were miserably hot and filthy from the train smoke coming through the window. In Los Angeles, they had a short layover and were then put on an old red streetcar in Long Beach and transferred to yet another train for the remainder of the trip to San Diego. Upon their arrival to the Marine Corps Operating Base, which predominantly served as the base for the Sixth Marine Regiment, the recruits received a very warm welcome from a very large and mean-looking Marine sergeant drill instructor. As Charles put it, "We were converted right there from raw civilian kids to the first phase of becoming Marines,"[4] and they remained there for eighteen months.

The recruits were issued 782 gear, which consisted of a cartridge belt, canteen, first-aid pack, belt suspender strap, and a tent, as well as a bucket issue which included a bar of yellow lye soap, scrub brush, razor, toothbrush, toothpaste, and other survival items. Also issued were blue denim bib overalls, all one size—enormously big and baggy. Charles reflected "that you could do an about face and the bibs would still be facing the same direction."[5] They were also issued a matching loose-fitting coat-style jacket. For footwear, each recruit received two pairs of comfortable high-top brown cordovan shoes, which took a good spit shine. Recruits were expected to have one pair of shoes for drill and work, and the other pair for inspection and dress shoes. They were issued one service uniform made of very heavy green kersey fabric and two pairs of trousers with narrowly tapered bottoms. Charles thought that the trousers never fit exactly right, and the bottoms were so tight they could not be put on or taken off without removing one's shoes. The coat was so tight in the shoulders that certain movements were difficult. These uniforms were miserably hot in the summertime, but they were the Liberty uniforms.

---

4   Transcript of recorded interviews of Charles L. Harrison by General Orlo K. Steele, USMC, retired, 2002.

5   Transcript.

If a recruit could not afford civilian clothing, this was the uniform that had to be worn on liberty all summer long.

Uniform "blues" were not issued unless a recruit was going to sea school. A recruit could purchase them at his own expense, but very few could afford them. Six months or so out of basic training, a Marine being discharged sold Charles his blues for a couple of dollars. Also issued to the recruits were khakis, canvas leggings, underwear, shirts, socks, and a helmet, as well as a Springfield .03 service rifle .30-caliber model 1903 (thirty-aught-six, or .30–06) and five or six rounds of ammunition. The Springfield rifle went into service in the Marine Corp in 1906. Training with the .03 rifle was conducted by the drill instructor at the rifle range, where they were also trained on the pistol and the Browning Automatic Rifle (BAR). With the rifle, they were required to fire ten rounds standing at the two-hundred-yard line. The three-hundred-yard line was for sitting, and then there was a rapid fire prone stage. The final stage was ten rounds prone from the five-hundred-yard line. Building 15 was the expeditionary storeroom, where they had everything needed to ship out a task force in a hurry.

The recruits were originally housed in old corrugated metal buildings with concrete floors, which they called the tin barracks. After boot camp, as the Marines were formed into the First Defense Battalion, they were moved into tents along the west side of the parade ground. At certain times there would be a Navy relief carnival set up on the parade grounds. At an early point in his career, the comedian

Red Skelton appeared at the Navy carnival, and Charles Harrison was thoroughly entertained by him there.

As they neared the end of basic training, most of the troops were hoping for orders to China. They were all fairly secluded in boot camp but somehow had heard that duty in China was the most desirable, and almost all the recruits wanted to go there. Sea duty was also a very attractive choice, but the recruits had to be in very good physical condition, and Charles did not think that he measured up. Charles Harrison came out of basic training as an infantryman with the rank of private. At that time, a private's pay rate was $20.80 a month, plus a clothing allowance.

In February of 1941, Charles Harrison was assigned to Pearl Harbor with the First Defense Battalion. The battalion was transported to Hawaii on the USS *Enterprise*. The hangar deck was completely full of guns and equipment, and there was a great deal of food aboard as well.

Once they arrived in Hawaii, Charles Harrison continued intensive military training but did have some spare time. Charles greatly admired a Marine sergeant named Brant, who was a lightweight boxer. He finally got up enough courage to approach Sergeant Brant, and Sergeant Brant took him to the base gym to work out with him and several other men from his outfit. The First Battalion had no boxing team, so bouts were arranged by a coach at the Marine barracks. Charles did fight a few bouts with crewmen off ships tied up in the harbor, but he was beaten up often and finally realized that this was not the right sport for him. There were many other things to do during liberty in Hawaii. Charles Harrison was seeing things he had only heard and read about during his childhood in Oklahoma. There were good movie theaters and restaurants, and occasionally a British ship would come into Pearl Harbor and the American Marines would entertain the Royal Marines from those ships.

In August, Charles and his fellow Marines were notified that they would be leaving Hawaii, and on August 18, 1941, Private Harrison boarded the Navy cargo ship *Regulus* with his detachment commander, Lieutenant Colonel Lewis A. Hohn, still unaware of his destination. The *Regulus* did not even have sleeping facilities. Lumber was brought aboard to build double-decker bunks in the cargo hold for the Marines. The food was not very good, and many of the men got seasick. The hatch covers were removed from the cargo holds where the men were sleeping in order to make the miserably hot nights bearable. Many of the men would take a blanket onto the deck to sleep. At some point en route, the junior officers were allowed to tell the troops that they were headed for Wake Island, which did not mean much to Private Harrison, as he did not even know where Wake Island was.

Wake, Midway, Johnston, and Palmyra Islands were all outposts protecting Hawaii, a vital staging area for war in the Pacific. Although actually atolls—tiny islands clustered on a reef-fringed lagoon—all four have been traditionally referred to as islands. The First Defense Battalion was divided among Pearl Harbor, Johnston, Palmyra, and Wake Islands.

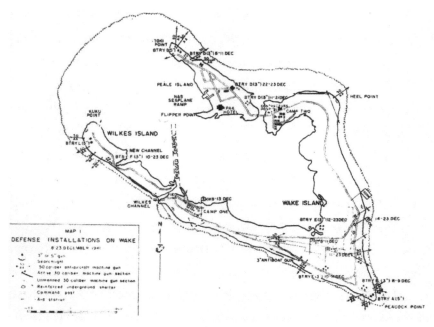

Wake Island

Upon arrival at Wake Island on August 18, 1941, Charles and the 171 Marines of his detachment, joined approximately one thousand civilian contractors already on Wake in establishing the defense of an advance Naval Air Station for PBY Amphibious Aircraft. Many of the young Marines with Charles did not understand the gravity of what lay ahead of them. They were gung ho, well-trained, and felt that they were ready for anything. As Charles put it, "The real details of what was happening diplomatically, and the real threat, I don't think I ever understood until the first bomb hit on Wake."[6]

---

[6]   Transcript.

Wake Island is a volcanically created arrangement of three separate islets (Peale, Wilkes, and Wake proper) that surround a central lagoon. Situated in the mid-Pacific about two thousand miles west of Hawaii, Wake is roughly six hundred miles closer to Tokyo than to Pearl Harbor. Owing to its location, part of the Japanese strategy called for the immediate seizure of Wake. Only by holding Wake could the Japanese prevent the United States from launching air attacks on Japanese bases on the Marshall and Gilbert Islands to the south. Wake Island is west of the international date line, which means it is always one day ahead of the United States.

Once the Marines arrived on Wake, their first task was to offload the heavy guns and supplies from the *Regulus*. Private Harrison remained on the *Regulus* until she was completely offloaded three days later. Once this had been accomplished, the Marines set up at camp 1, where there were rows of pyramid-shaped tents with wooden floors and an old tin mess hall that had originally been used by the civilian contractors on the island. The civilians had moved across the lagoon to camp 2, which seemed relatively luxurious in comparison to camp 1. The lagoon at Wake was blue and very tempting. The side of the Lagoon near camp 1 had been dredged to create a swimming area. There was no fresh water, so at that time, the only way to stay clean was to bathe in the saltwater lagoon or use the saltwater showers that had been rigged up near the swimming area.

Private Harrison's battery was deployed to Peale Island, with their battery commander Captain Bryghte D. "Dan"

Godbold. It took about fifteen minutes each day to drive in old trucks from camp 1, through the civilian camp 2, and cross a bridge to Peale Island to his gun position in Battery D. The five-inch naval guns were right on the tip of Peale Island and the three-inch anti-aircraft Marine battery gunners were about fifty yards back from them.

A portable coincidence range-finder is like those used at Wake Island in conjunction with the 5-inch/51 caliber guns of Batteries A, B, and L. It was believed that they had been removed from decommissioned and deactivated battleships in the 1920s.

Their new battalion commander, Major James P. S. Devereux, arrived on October 12, 1941. Upon his arrival, Major Devereux received clearance to read standing orders that authorized garrisons on the outlying islands to "open fire on all unidentified and suspicious aircraft" and stop all unauthorized vessels "from entering the Naval Defense Sea

Areas."[7] In response to the urgency of these orders, Major Devereux ordered that artillery ammunition be hauled out to every battery position, and he had a box of rifle ammunition placed in every tent in camp 1. The Marines under his direction worked from daylight to dark, sandbagging and getting the gun emplacements ready for action. Civilian contractors were also present getting the airfield in shape.

Major Devereux was a very strict regulation Marine, but he knew the hardships that his men were going through and the hard work they were doing. He recognized that they were in the tropics, and he allowed some leeway in the way his men dressed. He also did not require the usual physical exercise after early-morning reveille, because he realized they were all getting plenty of exercise as they worked.

Tensions between the United States and Japan were growing almost daily. If a Japanese task force menaced Wake, Devereux and his Marines intended to be ready for them. At that time, they did not realize that the Japanese were only eight hundred to nine hundred miles to the south in the Marshall Islands.

On October 24, 1941, B-17s started arriving at Wake while en route to bolster US defenses of the Philippine islands. Private Harrison and his fellow Marines took dozens of one-gallon cans from the mess hall and filled them with diesel or kerosene and a makeshift wick and then deployed them in a line along the sides of the runway to improve visibility for the aircraft's landing. The Marines

---

[7]   Gregory J. W. Urwin, *Facing Fearful Odds: The Siege of Wake Island*, 1997.

also had to take fifty-gallon drums with fuel for the B-17s and pump each barrel into each aircraft. It was a very slow and laborious process.

These were the first B-17 aircraft that Private Harrison had ever seen. He found out later that one of the pilots was Gene Jackson, an old childhood friend of his who had grown up in the same neighborhood and worked as a life-guard at Sand Springs Lake. Gene was later killed in the Philippines.

On October 29, 1941 the second contingent of the First Defense Battalion arrived on the USS *Castor* under the command of Major George H. Potter, who later became Major Devereux's executive officer. This contingent brought another 203 Marines to help garrison the island. Several of Private Harrison's close friends were in this second detachment. With this additional manpower, November was devoted to working on battery positions. At the same time, a number of the civilian contractors, who were barred from performing any uncontracted labor, began providing small doses of unofficial aid to the Marines.[8] Private Harrison thought that those civilians who assisted his battery were very good men and a great help, carrying ammunition, working on the gun crews, and passing ammunition to their loaders.

During the second week of November, a special Japanese envoy sent from Tokyo to help the Japanese ambassador in Washington deal with the Roosevelt administration, Saburo

---

[8]   Ibid.

Kurusu, passed through the island on a Pan American clipper. Private Harrison was aware that a Japanese dignitary had passed through but did not know the significance of it. By the end of November, war warnings were going out from Washington, DC, and Commander Winfield Scott Cunningham, USN, arrived on the 28th.

Commander Cunningham had been assigned to assume command of the Naval Air Station when it was ready to be commissioned. In the meantime, he was the senior officer on the island and nominally in command; however, the defense force functioned under the control of Major Devereux.

The men were so busy trying to prepare the fortifications that one day of filling and lifting sandbags and ammunition blended into the next. All that preparation and hard work was needed when, in December of 1941, Wake Island was bombarded by Japanese forces within a few hours after the attacks on Pearl Harbor. Officially, Wake Island was attacked on December 8, because of its position relative to the date line. Charles Harrison woke up early on the morning of December 8 and had hotcakes for breakfast. He later said, "I remember that very well, because it was the last good breakfast I had in a long while."[9]

Marine Gunner Harold C. Borth and PFC Johnson P. Holt climbed to the top of the camp's water tower to man

---

[9]   Matthew Renda, "A Veteran Recalls a Holiday on the Brink," *The Union*, Grass Valley, CA, December 23, 2011.

the observation post.[10] In those early days, radar was so new that it was not set up on Wake Island, so early warning was dependent upon keen eyesight. Right after breakfast, the bugler sounded "General Quarters," and all the men knew what that meant. They grabbed their weapons and headed to their battle stations. The gunnery sergeant, Jonathan Wright, gave orders to break out live ammunition, saying, "This is the real thing, guys. So you're going to get live ammunition and take good care of it... We don't know what's going to happen, but it's the real thing."[11]

Private Harrison's crew was put on trucks and taken out to their gun positions on Battery D. By that time, the word had gotten out that Pearl Harbor had been bombed and that this was not a drill. It was the real thing, and the Marines on Wake Island knew that they would probably be attacked next. They were right about that.

The crew members made their way to their guns and awaited the approaching Japanese fighter planes. A rain squall came up, and the low frequency hum of airplanes became audible as the bombers flew in at low altitude, right out of the raincloud. One of the crew, Kenny Marvin, said, "Look, the wheels are falling off their planes." Harrison replied, "You idiot, those are bombs."[12]

---

[10]   Gregory J. W. Urwin, *Facing Fearful Odds: The Siege of Wake Island*, 1997.

[11]   Transcript.

[12]   Matthew Renda, "A Veteran Recalls a Holiday on the Brink," *The Union*, Grass Valley, CA, December 23, 2011.

The first attack consisted of thirty-four land-based attack planes from Roi in the Marshall Islands. The attack caught all but three of Marine Fighter Squadron 211's Wildcat fighters on the ground and destroyed four of the eight aircraft. Fifty-seven military and civilian personnel were killed, and both of the twenty-five-thousand-gallon aviation fuel tanks were destroyed. The military encampments manned by Private Harrison and his fellow Marines were left relatively untouched on December 8 as the Japanese raid focused on the Pan American Airways facilities and the airstrip. Japanese attack planes were back on December 9 and 10, softening up the defenses of Wake Island prior to their invasion. On December 9 alone, Battery D's number 2 and 4 guns collectively fired one hundred rounds in response. At dawn on the morning of December 11, the Japanese returned with a naval task force consisting of three light cruisers, six destroyers, two patrol boats, and two armed merchantmen. The cruisers and destroyers shelled Wake for forty minutes, and having received no counterfire, they moved closer to the beach and attempted a landing mission with the hope of assuming control of this strategic point in the South Pacific.

Commanding Officer Major James Devereux did not immediately order return fire. He calmly and shrewdly considered the situation and concluded that his coastal defense guns were no match for the heavier armament of the attacking ships. His best tactic was to rely on the element of surprise and hope that the enemy would believe that the coast defense guns had been put out of action by the air raids. Once the ships were within 4,500 yards of the shore, Major Devereux launched his four remaining Wildcat fighters and ordered his shore batteries to commence firing. The Marines sank the Japanese destroyer *Hayate*, killing all of her 167-man crew, and damaged the destroyers *Oite* and *Mochizuki*. The destroyer *Kisaragi* was sunk, and the remaining ships were damaged. Although the attack was repelled, the battle was fierce. Batteries D and E fired a combined total of 225 rounds despite the fact that both batteries had only three guns that were still operational.[13] At one point in the battle, one of Private Harrison's crew members was killed. The Japanese pilots were fearless, and Private Harrison and many of the other Marines had a great deal of respect for them as military men.

Hoping to confuse the Japanese bombers, Major Devereux instructed Captain Godbold to move Battery D's three-inch anti-aircraft guns the length of Peale during the night of December 11.[14] He reconnoitered the new position selected by Major Devereux, and at 1745, after securing the battery positions, they began their shift. For the next eleven hours, Private Harrison and his fellow Marines, assisted by nearly two hundred fifty civilians, constructed new emplacements. By 0445 on December 12, Harrison's battery was again manned and ready, as Japanese aircraft

---

[13]   Arthur A. Poindexter, "Wake Island: America's First Victory," *Leatherneck*, December 1991.

[14]   John Wukovits, *The Battle for Wake Island*, 2003.

continued to attack Wake Island each day following their initial failure.[15]

Major Devereux was an extremely effective commander and a great morale booster. He did his best to ensure that both ammunition and hot food were delivered to his Marines. Even though communication was sketchy at best, the Marines on Wake Island were aware that the Philippines was also under attack.

During the day on December 15, Captain Godbold's men observed their usual routine, starting the day at full alert and replacing their natural camouflage before reducing the alert status at 0700. His men completed the shelters near the guns during the day, and at 1700, they stopped work to return to full alert. A half hour later, lookouts at Battery D reported a plane lurking among the low clouds to the east, and Captain Godbold reported the presence of the intruder to the island command post. Major Devereux concluded that what the lookouts spotted was a simple reconnaissance mission. He found out he was wrong when at 1800 eight Japanese flying boats came in at one thousand feet and dropped bombs on what they believed was the barracks area on the northern part of the island. They also strafed the area near Batteries D and B.[16]

The next day, December 16, Wake Island was raided at about 1330. American pilots spotted the incoming formations almost ten minutes before they reached the atoll. This

---

[15]   Gregory J. W. Urwin, *Facing Fearful Odds: The Siege of Wake Island*, 1997.

[16]   Ibid.

early warning information was passed to Captain Godbold, and Battery D was able to hurl ninety-five rounds skyward. It was estimated that four planes had been damaged, and one had crashed some distance from the island.[17]

On December 20, an aircraft from Hawaii piloted by Ensign J. H. J. Murphy and his copilot, Ensign Howard Ady, was able to land at Wake between air attacks. They delivered the news that they had been ordered to fly into Wake, an order so sensitive that Pearl Harbor hesitated to transmit it, lest the Japanese intercept it. They explained that a US Navy task force was on the way with reinforcements, ammunition, and replacement aircraft. The task force would evacuate the wounded and remove the 1,100 civilian contractors still on the island.[18] Morale soared with this news. However, instead of a US Navy task force, on December 23 the Japanese returned with six heavy cruisers, two aircraft carriers, fifty-four planes, and one thousand troops. At this point, Battery D possessed only two operational guns and no fire-control gear. Once again, the Wake Island Marines gave the United States something to cheer about, as they held off the invasion fleet for several hours, killing eight hundred Japanese in the process. But at 0230 on December 24, two Japanese landing craft beached on Wake Island. US Marines and Japanese grappled in hand-to-hand combat in the darkness. By 0300 Major Devereux and Commander Winfield Scott Cunningham, the senior commander on Wake Island, lost communications with

---

17   Ibid.
18   Ibid.

most of their scattered forces. Communication wires had been cut, and the radio network ceased to function. Eventually, the entire island was overrun, and at 0600, Commander Cunningham made the decision to surrender. Major Devereux began trying to get the surrender information to the Marines, who continued fighting until 1330. Eventually, Major Devereux carried out a white flag, and the Marines were told to put down their arms and come out.

Of the 449 Marines who manned Wake's defenses, 49 were killed, 32 were wounded, and the remainder became prisoners of war. Of the 68 Navy officers and men, 3 were killed, 5 wounded, and the rest were taken prisoner. The small five-man Army communications detachment suffered no fatalities, but all were taken prisoner.[19]

Of the 1,146 civilians involved in construction programs on Wake Island, 70 were killed, and 12 were wounded. With the exception of nearly 100 contractors who remained on Wake, the remainder of the civilians joined Wake's Marines, sailors, and soldiers in prisoner-of-war camps. The Japanese had lost two ships and almost a thousand men.[20]

It was at this point that the Wake Island defenders were able to see the Japanese naval infantry known as the Rik Sentai. Armed to the teeth, the Rik Sentai had their bayonets out and motioned the Marines to line up on the

---

[19]   Robert J. Cressman, *A Magnificent Fight: Marines in the Battle for Wake Island*, Marines in WWII Commemorative Series.

[20]   Ibid.

road. They were herded onto the runway, where they were made to strip down to their shoes. Their hands were tied behind their backs with communication wire, which was then looped around their necks, so if they lowered their hands, they would strangle themselves. The wire was then used to tie up the next Marine, and the next and the next. The Japanese had set up machine guns, loaded them, and aimed them at the Marines, who believed that they were about to be shot. After the prisoners had lain in the sun for several hours without water, Rear Admiral Sadamichi Kajioka, in a white uniform, came riding up the road on a bicycle, yelling, "Oye, oye, Chotamatay, chotamatay." He arrived for the formal surrender and gave orders that the prisoners were not to be executed. Later that day, the POWs were untied but left on the coral runway to blister and burn in the sun. Their wrists and necks were in terrible condition from the wire. They were organized into groups of fifty to one hundred and surrounded by machine guns. In the evening, when the sun went down, the POWs began to shiver from the abrupt temperature change.[21]

Major Devereux persuaded the Japanese to allow a detail of Marines to pick up the dead and bury them. When the work party returned, they reported that they had seen hundreds of Japanese bodies that the Japanese themselves were trying to remove. More Japanese forces were landing and looting the American supplies. Eventually, Private Harrison's group was taken to camp 2 and put into the

---

[21]   Transcript.

barracks. Major Devereux persuaded the Japanese to bring a fifty-gallon drum of water to the Marines. Unfortunately, the drum had previously contained gasoline, so the water had a foul taste. No food was given to the Marines for two to three days. The airfield had been armed with underground charges, and when the surrender order came, the charges were detonated so the Japanese would not be able to land airplanes on it. During this time, Private Charles Harrison feared for his life and was thinking to himself that "this is a helluva way to spend Christmas."[22]

On January 12, 1942 the prisoners of war, including Private Harrison, were herded to the beach, where they boarded the cargo hold of the Japanese hell ship *Nitta Maru* for transportation to Japan. Once they embarked, the POWs were cursed, kicked, and beaten with heavy bamboo clubs. The air in the holds was foul, bodies were stacked on bodies, and the heat was unbearable. Water was not provided, and men went mad for lack of it. On the second day, a routine was established whereby several buckets of a thin rice soup were lowered into the hold on ropes. Some days, a tiny fish head, scales and all, might be included in the pail. Dysentery became an epidemic, with many of the men so weak they could not even crawl to the slop buckets in the corner of the hold.

After several days of stifling heat, the temperature began to drop as the ship headed into the freezing mid-winter of northern Japan. After a six-day voyage into

---

[22] Matthew Renda, "A Veteran Recalls a Holiday on the Brink," *The Union*, Grass Valley, CA, December 23, 2011.

the near-freezing temperatures, the *Nitta Maru* reached Yokohama, Japan. In Yokohama, the officers and Major George H. Potter, the executive officer, were taken ashore for further interrogations. Five prisoners—two Marines, and three sailors—were brought on deck. In front of hundreds of Japanese onlookers, they were blindfolded, forced to kneel, and a guard chopped off their heads with a long sword. After the prisoners were beheaded, their bodies were mutilated by swords and bayonets. Once their captors were satisfied, their heads, body parts, and entrails were pushed over the edge of the dock.

From Yokohama, the *Nitta Maru* pulled anchor and headed toward Shanghai, China, arriving there on January 23, 1942. More prisoners were to be executed and mutilated at the Shanghai port in order to demonstrate Japanese superiority to the Chinese, but few people were at the dock to watch. Instead of being executed, the POWs were marched five miles through freezing temperatures to Woosung Prison Camp near Shanghai, arriving on January 24 with only the clothes on their backs. The temperature upon arrival at the camp was about fifteen degrees below zero.

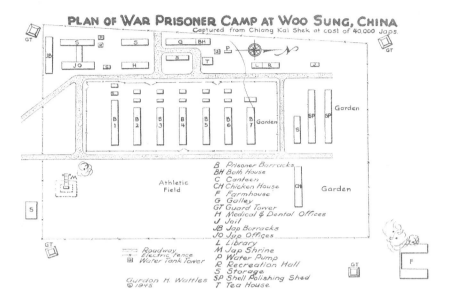

Diagram of WooSung Prison Camp

The internment camp was composed of wooden barracks formerly occupied by the Chinese and Japanese. There were defensive foxholes and trenches dug all around the perimeter of the camp. A guard tower stood at each end of the camp, and there was lighting along the perimeters. There was, however, no heat, no hot water, nor any toilets in the sleeping facilities. These sleeping facilities consisted of wooden shelves, with mattresses made of cloth bags filled with straw. Nine to ten men were assigned to each shelf and issued only a thin blanket. They slept as close to one another as they could in order to keep warm. The barracks were crudely wired for electricity. Outside the barracks was a wash rack with polluted water and a crude toilet which consisted of an oblong hole in the floor where the men would squat to relieve themselves. Food consisted of a scoop of rice three times a day with some occasional vegetable scraps. The Japanese gave them boiled water in wooden buckets, which they referred to as stick-and-berry tea. This "tea" looked like sweepings from the floors, but having been boiled, the prisoners felt it was safe to drink, as they would not have survived if they had to drink the polluted water from the wash rack. Each prisoner lost about sixty pounds during a year's captivity at Woosung Prison. The officers were put in similar wooden buildings but had separate rooms with only two to four officers to a room.

A Japanese sentry and an interpreter would come through the barracks every morning and every night to take roll call. The Marines were required to count off in Japanese—*itchi* (one), *ni* (two), *san* (three), and so forth—until everyone was accounted for. There were about 1,100 prisoners in the camp, which included Marines who had been captured from the Marine Legation Guard Force in North China and a few from the detachment that had been in Shanghai. When Private Harrison and his fellow Marines arrived at the internment camp at Woosung, it had no enclosure, but an electrified fence was later installed to deter escape attempts. Several men died on that fence, not trying to escape, but simply by touching it.

Commander Cunningham and Nathanial Daniel "Dan" Teters, the superintendent of the Wake Island civilian contractors, were imprisoned in the camp, along with Sir Mark Aitchison Young, Knight Commander of the Most Distinguished Order of Saint Michael and Saint

George and Governor-General of the British Crown colony of Hong Kong. Having been educated at Eton and Cambridge University, Mark Young entered the colonial service in 1909 but interrupted his career to put on a uniform during WWI. He assumed control of Hong Kong scarcely two months before twenty thousand Japanese troops descended on his ten-thousand-man garrison. Following seventeen days of resistance and the deaths of many British, Canadian, and Indian soldiers, Sir Mark surrendered. But the British statesman who entered Woosung gave no sign of being beaten. Tall and slender, Sir Mark bore himself with the dignity befitting his privileged background and position. The Japanese treated Sir Mark with a deference shown to no other prisoner at Woosung, providing him with two large rooms in one barrack, complete with an overstuffed chair, a real bed, and a radio. Sir Mark accepted these privileges, but he balked when the Japanese offered him better quality and larger quantities of food than the rest of the camp. This show of integrity won him the respect of the other POWs. The news-starved American POWs also appreciated that Sir Mark purposely played his radio loud enough that those standing outside his quarters could hear it. Sir Mark's status among the other prisoners grew when he continually chided the Japanese any time they violated the Geneva Convention.

The senior US Marine in the camp was Colonel William W. Ashurst, an impressive-looking individual who was probably the oldest Marine in the camp. Private

Harrison saw Colonel Ashurst only a few times when he was walking around the perimeter of the camp.

If any prisoner did something the Japanese considered to be wrong, everyone in the camp paid for it. A common punishment was for meals to be withheld from the prisoners. The Japanese also employed various types of torture, one of which was water torture, in which the Japanese would pour water in the prisoner's mouth while pinching their nose shut in an attempt to get information from them. Beatings were also very common.

The first permanent camp commander, Colonel Goichi Yuse, was a small man with a huge ego, who would walk around the camp, yelling "Kioski" (which means "attention") as he passed each group of prisoners. Colonel Yuse liked to gather the prisoners together to listen to his "speeches." He would scream and yell in Japanese, and on one occasion, his interpreter told the POWs that Colonel Yuse was going to provide a paper that everyone had to sign, promising that they would not try to escape. For some reason, Sir Mark Young was allowed to speak following Colonel Yuse, and he said, "The insipid little puke—don't anybody sign that thing. It wouldn't mean anything if you did, but don't do it."[23] The interpreter did not really understand what he was saying and allowed him to go on speaking.

On December 6, 1942, the Wake Island POWs were moved ten miles to Kiangwan, where they were used for

---

23   Transcript.

heavy labor on construction projects. The prisoners worked daily, constructing a rifle range approximately three to four miles from the Kiangwan Prison Camp, called the Fuji Project. On the way to the rifle range, the prisoners would pass through a number of Chinese villages. The Chinese had been told that the Marines were heathens and brought on evil spirits. The Chinese would beat on tin pans and shoot firecrackers to "scare the evil spirits away." The prisoners worked every day regardless of the weather conditions, which were miserable in the winter and very hot in the summer. The rifle range was below sea level, and the dirt was soft, so very often the digging would uncover graves. The digging was done with picks and shovels, and the dirt was then put into an ore cart that was moved down a track for dumping.

There was a particularly cruel and egotistical guard at the work site who constantly yelled at the POWs and threatened them with his bayonet. When the POWs would pull away from the digging area with a load of dirt to deliver for dumping, this guard would stand under an overhang to get out of the wind. On one occasion, the section leader of the work crew instructed the POWs to keep digging underneath the overhang so that when the guard moved under it, it might cave in on him. As the POWs pulled away with their load of dirt, the sentry moved under the overhang and was soon buried under tons of dirt. Other sentries ran up, and the POWs started digging, as though trying to rescue the guard, but they purposefully dug in the wrong places. When they finally uncovered the sentry, it was obvious to

Private Harrison that he was dead, but the POWs still made a show of trying to revive him. For their efforts to "save" this sentry, several days later the POWs were given a gift of a small package of moldy cigarettes.[24]

Japanese treatment was brutal at every location and during every movement of the POWs. Many POWs were beaten with heavy objects. Some were hung by their heels. Their noses were broken so they could not breathe through their noses, and then water was forced through their mouths until they suffocated. It became common for prisoners to be put on display in front of their fellow POWs. Their noses and teeth would be smashed with heavy clubs. If the prisoner moved during this ordeal, he would be smashed again as punishment for moving. If he fell, he would be pushed back onto his feet and receive more punishment, and when he could no longer stand, the POW would be lashed to a pole. The guards would change shifts, but the POW beatings continued around the clock.

Along with beatings, hunger and starvation were common. In describing his experiences, Private Harrison said, "In China, where I was confined by the Japanese after the fall of Wake during WWII, I had known the meaning of real hunger for the first time. I remembered vivid dreams of delicious food and of waking with saliva drooling from my mouth and a steady gnawing pain in my stomach. I thought of how the conversation had always turned to food during those hungry weeks, no matter what the opening conver-

---

[24] Transcript.

sation had been. Peanut butter and hotcakes monopolized the talk then."[25]

Private Harrison recalled that the Japanese instructed the officers to form a work party and create a sizeable vegetable garden just outside the main gate. The garden was over an acre wide and produced some very nice vegetables for the Japanese. The most prized items that came out of that garden went to the camp commander, Colonel Yuse. Colonel Yuse particularly enjoyed the watermelons. After he died suddenly one summer, the rumor circulated through the camp that two of the doctors (Dr. Kahn and Dr. Foley) had injected a deadly virus into the largest and most beautiful watermelon in the garden, because they knew that it would go to Colonel Yuse. Private Harrison and the other prisoners secretly hoped that this story was true, as they felt it was an end that Colonel Yuse well deserved.[26]

Jimmy James was an American who owned a restaurant along the Bund in Shanghai. He had been a familiar figure there prior to the war and appeared to have some influence with the Japanese, as they allowed him to provide the prisoners with a complete meal during the holidays in 1942. Private Harrison remembered this meal as being "everything—it was turkey, the dressing, the whole bit. It was just unbelievable, and we all wondered how could an American, as much as the Japanese hated Americans, be able to do this? But there it was, and you'd never forget it,

---

25   Charles L. Harrison, "Twice across the Rainbow," USMC, *US Naval Institute Proceedings*, vol. 78, no. 5, May 1952.

26   Transcript.

because we were really hungry and it was just a complete holiday meal." [27]

During his time at Camp Kiangwan, Private Harrison heard rumors that the United States had launched a counteroffensive. One of the other prisoners, Lieutenant Kinney, had made a crystal set and was able to get some outside news. He would share what he learned, characterizing the information as rumors so that the Japanese would not know where it came from. The information the prisoners received was vague, but they did believe that things were going well for the United States in the Pacific. As the war progressed, the treatment by the Japanese became increasingly more vicious.

It was difficult for the prisoners to keep track of time during their incarceration. Private Harrison rarely knew what day or week it was, but he knew roughly the months and years. Sometime in 1944, Private Harrison was allowed to send his family a letter from the prison camp. The letter was dated April 12, 1944, and in it, Private Harrison wrote to his family: "Several of my comrades from in and near Tulsa are still here... We've been together a long time, as most of us were in the battalion a year or two before it left the States in early 1941. As far as we are concerned, there is not a finer officer, soldier, and gentleman anywhere than our skipper Major Devereux. I should like to believe that you accept all this as we do. Tough breaks are something that must be accepted and endured. I consider it very small

---

[27]   Transcript.

payment and sacrifice for eighteen years of happiness back there in God's own country with you. I think you know my nature well enough to see that I don't like to think of you worrying or grieving for me. I want you to be free and happy so that I can think of you that way, as I do, and share it with you even from here. As for my health, I have had only a few days' illness during these past two years. I remember when I was a kid someone told me that my dad was as strong and tough as a buffalo. Perhaps I inherited a tough constitution from him, or maybe I am just fortunate, but comparatively, I have been very healthy. Take care of yourselves and keep smiling. Charles."[28]

The Kiangwan compound was located between two Japanese airfields, and the same year that Private Harrison wrote that letter to his family, sometime in 1944, he recalled seeing P-51s engaging the enemy. He could hear the .50-caliber machine guns open up and their bombs detonate nearby. The P-51s would dip their wings as they passed overhead as a sign that they knew the prisoners were there. During this exchange, Private Harrison witnessed a P-51 engage two Japanese bombers. One of the bombers exploded, and the tail gunner was separated from the plane and fell to the ground. The other bomber seemed to completely disintegrate in the air. Private Harrison was inspired by what he saw and remembered this as being a great day, despite the fact that he was being goosed along at the point

---

[28]   Letter from Charles Harrison, April 12, 1944, courtesy of Jane Harrison Williams.

of a Japanese bayonet to return to the barracks while he witnessed these exchanges.

In May of 1945, the Japanese decided to close the camp in which Private Harrison was imprisoned and move the remaining prisoners to the north and eventually to the home islands. The prisoners were moved in cattle cars after finishing the Fuji rifle range project. The cattle cars had straw on the decks, and there was some room to lay down, but they were very crowded. The rail cars traveled north following the Yangtze River as far as Nanking.

During this train ride, Lieutenant Jim McBrayer from Muleshoe, Texas, led several other officers in an escape attempt. Lieutenant McBrayer had been stationed in North China before the war to study the Chinese language, history, and geography. Therefore, he spoke some Mandarin Chinese, and he knew the landmarks near Nanking. He chose an area along the train route that would afford the greatest likelihood for success. The officers were able to work some screws loose on the bars over a small window in the back of the train car. A five-gallon can had been placed in the officers' train car for the purpose of relieving themselves, and the Japanese had allowed the officers some privacy by hanging a blanket in the corner of the car in front of the *benjo* toilet. At night, one by one, the officers were able to escape through the small window behind the blanket and regroup.

By daylight, the Japanese realized the officers had made an escape. They unloaded the entire train and subjected all the prisoners to long-winded ranting speeches in

Japanese. Private Harrison recalled hearing rumors that the Japanese officer in charge of this transfer of prisoners was so upset with the loss of face that he placed himself under arrest. After this escape, the remainder of the prisoners were taken to Fengtai, a railroad yard about fifteen miles outside of Peking, where they spent several weeks quartered in an old warehouse called a godown in Chinese. During their time in Fengtai, the prisoners were assigned to work parties. The main gate to the compound was often open, and on one occasion, a caravan of camels passed by the open gate, and one baby camel got loose inside the compound. The Japanese were screaming and agitated, as they had to allow some of the camel herders into the compound to round up the baby. Some of the prisoners were looking at the baby camel as dinner, but it was ultimately returned to its mother. This distraction was the only entertainment afforded to the prisoners during their entire stay.[29]

Private Harrison's Japanese had improved after his many years of imprisonment, and he was able to somewhat communicate with the guards at Fengtai. They were friendlier and less vicious than any of the previous guards with whom he had come into contact. After several weeks in Fengtai, Charles Harrison and his fellow prisoners were loaded onto a train which headed north to Mukden, Manchuria, and then crossed into North Korea, where they were put on passenger trains with all of the windows blacked out. Trying to peek out of those windows was con-

---

[29]   Transcript.

sidered to be a great offense and would have resulted in being stabbed by a bayonet or beaten.

The men were crowded three to a seat, so they had to take turns sleeping. Although they had some small amounts of food provided to them, the prisoners were always hungry through this trip, which turned out to be along the entire length of Korea. Eventually, the prisoners ended up in Pusan, Korea.

Disembarking in Pusan during a rainstorm, the prisoners were taken to open sheds, which were storage facilities right on the docks. The weather broke after a day or two, but it was cold and miserable in those sheds. The prisoners were then divided into work parties and given what were called *yaho* poles, a long bamboo pole with a straw basket slung in the middle. With one man on each end, they were taken to an area where tons of raw salt was piled up. The salt was shoveled into the yaho basket until it weighed one hundred pounds or more and then carried by the prisoners approximately one hundred yards up the gangplank of a ship and dumped into an open hold. This was repeated all day. The shoulders of the prisoners were worn raw from the many trips with the heavy loads. After a week of this intense labor, the prisoners were loaded onto a ship headed to Honshu, Japan. No water was provided to the prisoners during this transport. There were overhead steam pipes in the holds where the prisoners were kept and the men would take turns lying underneath the steam pipes, catching the drips of condensation in their mouths. Those few drops provided the only fresh water they had for the duration of the trip.

The men were taken to shore on the west coast of Honshu. They were put onto trains in the fishing village of Sosa, Japan, for transport to Tokyo. Once again, the windows of the train were covered, and the prisoners were forbidden to peek out. When they arrived in the bustling city of Tokyo, they were immediately led underground into a subway, where the boom and thud of bombing raids could be heard. The crowds of Japanese civilians taking refuge in the subway began to beat on the prisoners and throw things at them, so their guards hustled them quickly onto the subway cars. As the door to a car would open, the guards would shove prisoners inside. The doors would slam shut, and they would wait for the next car and do the same. One of the prisoners, a sergeant, was being severely beaten with an umbrella by a Japanese civilian. This Sergeant happened to be the last person shoved into his subway car before the door slammed shut, and he turned himself around quickly, grabbed the Japanese civilian by the tie, and held onto the necktie as the door shut. He continued holding onto the tie and the Japanese civilian outside the door attached to that tie until the train took off, and he did not let go until the train was outside of the station. It was a high price to pay for flogging a Marine.[30]

The prisoners traveled across Tokyo on the subway, and when they disembarked, they were hurried onto a

---

[30] Transcript.

steam train. They knew that they were heading north, but once again, the windows of the train were covered. At the northern tip of Honshu, Private Harrison boarded a ferry. Aboard that ferry, the prisoners were give a ration of grasshopper that appeared to have been deep cooked in soy sauce. Reluctantly, the hungry prisoners ate the grasshoppers and were surprised to find that they actually tasted good. Upon disembarking from the ferry, the prisoners were also provided a rice ration. They were then put on another train and taken further north, into Hokkaido. Private Harrison and his fellow prisoners hiked ten or fifteen miles into the mountains to a coal mining area in a little village called Utashinai-mura—*mura* meaning "village," and Utashinai, the name of the village. They were herded through this village into a small camp, populated by Wake Island Marine POWs.

Most of the Wake Island POWs that survived the first year in China were moved to Osaka, Japan, and then to various work camps in the Tokyo and Yokohama area. A great many of the POWs had died in captivity or were executed, as was recorded after the war.

The camp on the Japanese island of Hokkaido, in which Private Harrison found himself, was surrounded by an eight-foot board fence, and the buildings themselves were in fairly good condition. There, he was reunited with Marine Major James Devereux and many of his fellow First Defense Battalion Marines and Wake Island sailors, as well as several Marines and sailors captured in China. Along with Korean prisoners, the American POWs worked as slave laborers in the coal mines of the Hokkaido Shipping and Mining Company, which controlled all the mines in that area. The Korean prisoners worked in two mines, while the American POWs operated a third drift mine, which had been abandoned for twenty years. The mine had some type of fungus growing on the overhead, and it was wet and sloshy as the men dug the coal with picks and shovels. The men would work ten-hour shifts in the mines, during which time their feet were always wet. The Japanese themselves would not go into the mine, so some Korean prisoners were used as supervisors. By this time, the POWs had some sense that the war was moving in favor of the Allies. The Korean "supervisors" spoke Japanese and carried their rice ration with them wrapped in Japanese newspapers. The prisoners would take the newspapers that the Koreans had thrown away after eating the rice, stuff them into their clothing, and then read them once they returned to camp.

The Japanese required every prisoner to stand up and bow or salute to every member of the guard whenever they passed by, and if the prisoner was too slow to do this, the guards would beat him. Prisoners were also beaten simply because they could not understand the Japanese language, so Private Harrison had learned to read and speak Japanese as a survival tactic, and it was in this manner that he could read about the progress of the war, and he learned that an atomic bomb had been dropped on Hiroshima.

By this point in the war, most of the prisoners were on the brink of starvation and death. Many of them believed that if the war had lasted even another month, they would not have survived. It was not until after the bombing of Hiroshima that the cruelest prison guards were replaced with Japanese guards that were friendlier, and things in the camp began to change dramatically. There was no more heavy work for the POWs, and some villagers were allowed to bring gifts and food to the prisoners. A gracious Japanese gave the prisoners a live mule, which they were allowed to butcher and eat.

Within days of the bombing of Hiroshima, the prisoners were allowed to put some letters on top of the roof that spelled out "US POWs." In late August of 1945, US Navy aircraft airdropped fifty-five-gallon drums crammed with food, medicine, and clothing to the prisoners. The drums would explode open when they hit the ground. The supply drums were put together so quickly that the Navy personnel did not realize they were a danger, as well as a lifesaver, to the men on the ground. At least one Wake Island Marine was killed by a falling metal drum. Once the pilots realized what was happening, they discontinued the dangerous drops, but enough American food and medical supplies had been delivered to care for the prisoners.[31]

Once the atomic bomb had fallen on Hiroshima, the Japanese guards gave up their control, and Private Harrison believed they were not even armed. Several of the Marines made a run for the fence, jumped up, and went over the top. The guards did not react, so the men just laughed and returned to camp through the gate. The officers rejoined

---

[31]   John Wukovits, *The Battle for Wake Island,* 2003.

the other prisoners when it became obvious that the war was over. Major Devereux gathered the men together and told them he was very proud of the way they had conducted themselves throughout their imprisonment. On September 9, 1945, the First Cavalry Division reached Hokkaido and liberated Charles Harrison and his fellow prisoners.

Once the American Army troops arrived, the Marines were taken to the nearest train station. They were then taken by rail to an airfield near Hokkaido, where US aircraft C-47s awaited them. The Marines were flown to Honshu, Japan. Once aboard the aircraft, the pilot flew over Tokyo so that the Marines could see the massive ruins below them. In Yokohama, they were taken aboard an American ship, and a massive storm hit the harbor in Tokyo. When the storm subsided, the Marines set sail for Guam, where they were admitted to Fleet Hospital 103. The galley was open to the Marines day and night, and the cook would prepare anything they wanted. Most of the men got sick from eating too much until they recovered some weight. Private Harrison's weight had dropped to less than 110 pounds, and his shoulder blades and ribs protruded from his body. He had contracted malaria during his imprisonment, and many of his fellow Marines had contracted beriberi. The staff, nurses, and corpsmen at Fleet Hospital 103 provided good and compassionate medical care, plenty of food, and vitamins to the men. Private Harrison gained about ten pounds during his first week there. The Red Cross was on hand to relay messages from the Marines to their families back home. From Fleet Hospital 103, PFC

Harrison was taken by ship to Hawaii. After a short lay-over in Honolulu, he was transported to Oak Knoll Naval Hospital in Oakland, California.

Private Harrison received excellent treatment at Oak Knoll Hospital, where he was issued uniforms and given liberty and some back pay. Never much of a drinker, Private Harrison enjoyed having a few beers, some good restaurant food, and traveling in a taxicab with some money in his pocket.

While on liberty, PFC Harrison went to the Yankee Doodle Bar in San Francisco, where he met fellow Marines who had also been in combat. The stories they shared about Iwo Jima and Peleliu made his jaw drop. From Oak Knoll Naval Hospital in California, PFC Harrison was sent to the naval hospital nearest his home town, which was in Norman, Oklahoma, near Oklahoma City. He stayed in that hospital but was allowed generous convalescent leaves. He was paid back pay, at one time getting a check for $1,200, which made him feel like a wealthy man.

Charles Harrison made the decision to stay in the Marine Corps as he realized that now that the war was over, there would be hundreds of thousands of discharged sol-diers, sailors, and Marines looking for work. He decided to remain with the Marines with the goal of becoming a gunnery sergeant. Once he was judged fully recovered and fit for duty, he was promoted to corporal and then to buck sergeant, and was sent to a Marine detachment in Norman, Oklahoma.

Returning to his hometown on leave, Charles Harrison found his childhood sweetheart, Mary Hogan, patiently waiting for him. They became engaged immediately, and after his assignment as a sergeant to a base police office in San Diego, California, he sent for Mary. Charles Harrison and Mary Hogan were married on June 17, 1946, in a traditional military wedding beneath the crossed sabers of the honor guards in the Marine Corps Base Chapel at the Marine Corp Recruit Depot in San Diego. Commander W. A. Mahler, a Catholic chaplain, officiated at the ceremony. Captain John Hamas gave the bride away. Captain Hamas and all six men of the honor guard were POWs who had served with Charles Harrison.

Charles, whose father has a Methodist Church in Oklahoma named in his honor, converted to the Roman Catholic faith of his new Irish wife, was baptized on April 1, 1947, and settled in to married life. He and his bride were able to procure a naval housing unit near Old Town, San Diego, which was their first home together.

Working for the base police office was a good job with good hours for the new husband. Sergeant Harrison had a big car and was enjoying this first year of freedom, during which he and 492 other Marines received the Presidential Unit Citation for the defense of Wake Island, which earned the battalion the nickname of Wake Island Defenders. He had been promoted to staff sergeant, which meant a small increase in pay. He and Mary had just welcomed their first child, Patrick, who was born at North Island Naval Air

Station on Coronado Island in California on May 7, 1947, when Sergeant Harrison received orders to Midway Island. He escorted Mary and their son back to Tulsa, Oklahoma, before reporting to Midway. Mary and Patrick would be staying with Mary's Aunt Stella, who had helped raise Mary and her sisters when her mother had died at a young age. Mary's two sisters lived close by, so Sergeant Harrison felt confident that his wife and child would be well cared for in his absence.

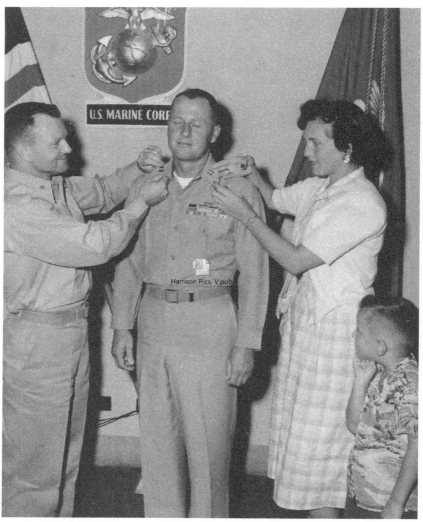

Mary Harrison pinning Captain bars on Charles Harrison.

NAVY COMMENDATION: Major Charles L. Harrison (left) is presented the Navy Commendation Medal with Combat "V" by Major General Robert E. Cushman Jr., Camp Pendleton Base Commander Feb. 7. Maj. Harrison earned the medal while serving as Executive Officer of the 2nd Battalion, 3rd Marine Regiment in Vietnam from December 1965 to Aug. 1966. He was cited for displaying outstanding leadership during an amphibious landing and in operations Double Eagle and Liberty. (OFFICIAL U. S. MARINE CORPS PHOTO)

Charles L. Harrison

Charles and Mary Harrison

THE WHITE HOUSE
WASHINGTON

5 December, 1945.

Dear Charles L. Harrison,

It gives me special pleasure
to welcome you back to your native
shores, and to express, on behalf of
the people of the United States, the
joy we feel at your deliverance from
the hands of the enemy. It is a
source of profound satisfaction that
our efforts to accomplish your return
have been successful.

You have fought valiantly
and have suffered greatly. As your
Commander in Chief, I take pride in
your past achievements and express
the thanks of a grateful Nation for
your services in combat and your
steadfastness while a prisoner of war.

May God grant you happiness
and a successful future.

Harry Truman

THIS IS AN IMPORTANT RECORD
SAFEGUARD IT.

1. LAST NAME-FIRST NAME-MIDDLE NAME	2. SERVICE NUMBER	3. SOCIAL SECURITY NUMBER		
HARRISON, Charles Lee	058833	440	16	1172

4. DEPARTMENT, COMPONENT AND BRANCH OR CLASS	5a. GRADE, RATE OR RANK	5b. PAY GRADE	6. DATE OF RANK		
U. S. Marine Corps	LtCol	N/A	DAY 04	MONTH Oct	YEAR 67

7. U. S. CITIZEN	8. PLACE OF BIRTH (City and State or Country)	9. DATE OF BIRTH		
☑ YES ☐ NO	Tulsa, Oklahoma	DAY 21	MONTH Mar	YEAR 21

10a. SELECTIVE SERVICE NUMBER	b. SELECTIVE SERVICE LOCAL BOARD NUMBER, CITY, COUNTY, STATE AND ZIP CODE	c. DATE INDUCTED		
Not Available	Not Available	DAY MONTH YEAR Not Applicable		

11a. TYPE OF TRANSFER OR DISCHARGE	b. STATION OR INSTALLATION AT WHICH EFFECTED
Retired	MB,USNWS,SB,FA,Fallbrook, California 92028

c. REASON AND AUTHORITY CMC ltr DMA-pjg-17 of 21 April 1969	d. EFFECTIVE DATE		
Tr Ret'd List 10 USC 6323; SN 760	DAY 31	MONTH Jul	YEAR 69

12. LAST DUTY ASSIGNMENT AND MAJOR COMMAND	13a. CHARACTER OF SERVICE	b. TYPE OF CERTIFICATE ISSUED
MB,USNWS,SB,FA,Fallbrook, California	HONORABLE	N/A

14. DISTRICT, AREA COMMAND OR CORPS TO WHICH RESERVIST TRANSFERRED	15. REENLISTMENT CODE
Not Applicable	N/A

16. TERMINAL DATE OF RESERVE/ UMT&S OBLIGATION	17. CURRENT ACTIVE SERVICE OTHER THAN BY INDUCTION	b. TERM OF SERVICE (Years)	c. DATE OF ENTRY		
DAY MONTH YEAR Not Applicable	a. SOURCE OF ENTRY ☐ ENLISTED (First Enlistment) ☐ ENLISTED (Prior Service) ☑ OTHER AcDu as Commissioned Officer ☐ REENLISTED	05	DAY MONTH YEAR Jun 64		

18. PRIOR REGULAR ENLISTMENTS	19. GRADE, RATE OR RANK AT TIME OF ENTRY INTO CURRENT ACTIVE SVC	20. PLACE OF ENTRY INTO CURRENT ACTIVE SERVICE (City and State)
Three (3)	Major	Quantico, Virginia

21. HOME OF RECORD AT TIME OF ENTRY INTO ACTIVE SERVICE (Street, RFD, City, State and ZIP Code)	22. STATEMENT OF SERVICE	YEARS	MONTHS	DAYS
5577 Via Bello Street, San Diego, San Diego, California 92111	(1) NET SERVICE THIS PERIOD	05	01	02
	CREDITABLE FOR BASIC PAY PURPOSES (2) OTHER SERVICE	24	09	10
23a. SPECIALTY NUMBER & TITLE / b. RELATED CIVILIAN OCCUPATION AND D.O.T. NUMBER	(3) TOTAL (Line (1) plus Line (2))	29	10	12
0302 / 0-68.24 Forester	b. TOTAL ACTIVE SERVICE	25	10	12
Inf Officer / Aide (gov ser)	c. FOREIGN AND/OR SEA SERVICE	09	10	00

24. DECORATIONS, MEDALS, BADGES, COMMENDATIONS, CITATIONS AND CAMPAIGN RIBBONS AWARDED OR AUTHORIZED
Bronze Star Medal w/combat V   Asiatic-Pacific Medal w/1 satr
Purple Heart Medal   World War II Victory Medal
Good Conduct Medal w/3 stars   Navy Presidential Unit Citation w/2 stars
American Defense Service Medal   Marine Corps Expedition Medal w/silver W   See Remarks

25. EDUCATION AND TRAINING COMPLETED
High School - 12
Recruiters School
Amphibious Warfare School

26a. NON-PAY PERIODS/TIME LOST (Preceding Two Years)	b. DAYS ACCRUED LEAVE PAID	27. a. INSURANCE IN FORCE (NSLI or USGLI)	b. AMOUNT OF ALLOTMENT	c. MONTH ALLOTMENT DISCONTINUED
	60	☐ YES ☑ NO	$ N/A	N/A
	28. VA CLAIM NUMBER	29. SERVICEMEN'S GROUP LIFE INSURANCE COVERAGE		
None	c. N/A	☑ $10,000 ☐ $5,000 ☐ NONE		

30. REMARKS
Korean Service Medal w/2 stars   Navy Commendation Medal
UN Service Medal   Presidential Unit Citation 4th Award
National Defense Service Medal w/1 star   Combat Action Ribbon
Korean Presidential Unit Citation   Viet Nam Campaign Medal w/device
Viet Nam Service Medal w/3 stars

31. PERMANENT ADDRESS FOR MAILING PURPOSES AFTER TRANSFER OR DISCHARGE (Street, RFD, City, County, State and ZIP Code)	32. SIGNATURE OF PERSON BEING TRANSFERRED OR DISCHARGED
Route 2, Box 1825, Grass Valley, California 95945	*Charles L. Harrison*

33. TYPE NAME, GRADE AND TITLE OF AUTHORIZING OFFICER	34. SIGNATURE OF OFFICER AUTHORIZED TO SIGN
W. R. M. TUCKER, USMC ExecO	*W. R. M. Tucker*

DD FORM 214 MC (1900)   PREVIOUS EDITIONS OF THIS FORM ARE OBSOLETE   ARMED FORCES OF THE UNITED STATES   REPORT OF TRANSFER OR DISCHARGE   S/N-0101-880-4301

Certified True Copy   *Charles L. Harrison, Lt.Col. 058833 USMC*

Captain Charles L. Harrison

Marine T/Sgt. Charles L. Harrison whose wife Mrs. Mary P. Harrison lives at 801 North Elwood St., Tulsa, Oklahoma spends his first day with American forces since last December when he was captured by Chinese Reds during the 1st Marine Division's savage battle in the Chosin Reservoir. Harrison was a captive of the Japanese for three and a half years in WWII. He says he feels "as though I am becoming a professional prisoner of war." The Harrisons have two sons, Pat aged 4 and Mike, ages 8 months. (OFFICIAL U. S. MARINE CORPS PHOTOGRAPH)

LEO AIME LABRIE

COMMANDER NAVAL FORCES FAR EAST
PHOTOGRAPHIC LABORATORY
TELEPHONE 26-7211 EXT 221

MARINE'S RETURN

31 MAY 1951

Recounting their experiences with Chinese Reds are (left to
right) S/Sgt James B. Nash of 1114 9th St., Durham, NC;
T/Sgt Charles L. Harrison of 801 N. Elwood St, Tulsa, Okla.;
PFC John A. Haring of 532 W. Chumang St., Painted Post, NY;
Army Cpl. Saburo Shimomura, of 2915 Pingtree Ave., Ogden , Utah;
and Cpl. Paul R. Witmer of 232 Main St., Hemeville, Pa.
Cpl. Witmer is asking the released Chinese Red-held prisoners
about their experiences in walking over 800 miles thru North
Korea for the past 6 months after having been captured by
the Chinese in the Chosin Reservoir area last December while
fighting with the 1st Marine Division.
RELEASE: U S MARINE CORPS PHOTO - IF PUBLISHED PLEASE CREDIT
OFFICIAL U S MARINE CORPS PHOTOGRAPH

NOTE: RELEASED VIA U S NAVY RADIPHOTO 28 MAY

Bronze Star Medal W/v For Valor is worn to denote combat heroism or to recognize individuals who are exposed to personal hazard during direct participation in combat operations.

Small ceramics found by Charles Harrison while digging to construct a rifle range outside of Kiangwan Prison Camp

THE KOREAN EXPERIENCE

After a year and a half in San Diego, Sergeant Harrison received orders for reassignment to the base on Midway Island in the Pacific, where he was assigned to a 90 millimeter anti-aircraft unit. Family quarters were being constructed at the time of his arrival. Once the enlisted family quarters were completed, Sergeant Harrison's wife and son were able to rejoin him. Because the enlisted family quarters were brand-new and nicely furnished, the quality of life was good, and he and Mary enjoyed being able to walk along the beach with their infant son. The young family enjoyed this idyllic lifestyle until June of 1950, when Staff Sergeant Harrison was sent to Camp Lejeune at Courthouse Bay, in Jacksonville, North Carolina.

In North Carolina, the Harrison family was living in a housing complex of cinderblock buildings called Holly Ridge, about fifteen miles from Camp Lejeune. The units were small one-bedroom apartments heated with coal. Water had to be heated over a coal fire cook stove, as there was no running hot water. Sergeant Harrison did not have a car in North Carolina and, therefore, had to carpool or hitchhike into Camp Lejeune. During this period, Charles Harrison would often have nightmares about his prisoner-of-war experience. He would sometimes find himself sitting straight up in bed, speaking Japanese, and this frightened Mary, who did not really understand what was happening to her husband.

As 1950 progressed, Sergeant Harrison was able to move his family out of Holly Ridge and into military housing in an area called Midway Park, which was a great improvement. It was a good life until the morning of Sunday, June 25, 1950, when ninety thousand North Korean troops pushed across the Thirty-Eighth Parallel and came south. Sergeant Harrison was a military policeman and an investigator at this time, and almost overnight, all dependents had to be moved from Camp Lejeune. He again was forced to put his now-pregnant wife and small child on a train headed back to Oklahoma before he himself was shipped by train from Camp Lejeune to Camp Pendleton near San Diego, as a squad leader in the Second Combat Service Group.

Much activity was apparent at Camp Pendleton. Divisions were being formed, troops were coming and going, and units were being combined. Staff Sergeant Harrison was moved by truck to the port in San Diego, where he boarded the *George Clymer*, an amphibious troop ship, for a long hot journey across the Pacific Ocean to the South China Sea.

General Douglas MacArthur, United Nations supreme commander, had conceived of the idea to land at the strategic port of Inchon in July of 1950. He had to vigorously sell the idea to every senior military commander in the Far Eastern theater. The extreme tidal conditions at Inchon made for a very risky landing. There were only six hours each day in which the tide permitted access to the landing areas. It was determined that the only possible dates when the highest tides were available were September 15, October 11, and November 3. The Marines also regarded the Inchon landing site as particularly hazardous as it necessitated landing right in the middle of the city.

Despite the risks, General MacArthur was confident of his success. Inchon was quite a prize, as an invasion force there would sit astride the principal supply routes to the south, permit the capture of the best airfield in South Korea, cut off and isolate most of the North Korean Army fighting to the south, and possibly recapture Seoul. General MacArthur's persistence ultimately changed the course of the war.

On September 15, 1950, US Marine forces, including Staff Sergeant Harrison aboard the *George Clymer*, made a surprise amphibious landing at Inchon, on the west coast of Korea. Nature cooperated with the Marines that day, as September 15 was clear, with the wind at six knots from the northeast. The Marines on the *George Clymer* made what is called a wet-shoe amphibious landing close to the beach at Inchon, where they literally waded through the mud to shore. Staff Sergeant Harrison was put in charge of North Korean POWs in an old nail factory close to the beach at Inchon. The frontline troops were sending prisoners back to the nail factory, so Sergeant Harrison and his men hastily made a barbwire enclosure within it. They gathered the prisoners there until an interrogator and interpreter could interview them and sort them out, transporting the prisoners they felt might have some information to another location for further interrogation. Japan occupied Korea for forty years, so the North Koreans spoke Japanese. Harrison's company commander was aware that Charles Harrison also spoke some Japanese and explained to him that was why he was put in charge of these North Korean prisoners.

Unbeknownst to both Sergeant Harrison and his company commander, General MacArthur had come ashore. In a jeep, he drove to the frontlines, filled with compliments for the Marines, who in turn gawked with surprise to see the five-star general striding about the front, laughing and cracking jokes. As soon as Sergeant Harrison recognized General MacArthur approaching the nail factory, he turned toward the prisoners and called them to attention in Japanese. He could hear the whispers among the prisoners, "Macassa, Macassa," which meant "MacArthur" to them. Despite having his back turned, he could hear General MacArthur speaking to his company commander, saying "Treat 'em well, but work them hard." The Marines actually had no intention of working these prisoners; they simply wanted to sort them out to find those who could provide information.[32]

---

[32]   Transcript.

Peardale resident Charles Harrison stands guard over some 200 North Korean prisoners shortly after the 1950 landing at Inchon North Korea, Gen. Douglas MacArthur is in background. Harrison was taken prisoner by the North Koreans a few weeks after this photograph was taken.

Picture from Life Magazine October 2, 1950

After the recapture of Seoul from the communists, Staff Sergeant Harrison was assigned to a prison in Seoul, guarding North Korean prisoners. The prison was very large with a brick enclosure and many cells, so it was much easier to secure the prisoners than it had been at the nail factory in Inchon.

In October of 1950, the First Marine Division embarked on an amphibious mission, steaming around the east coast of Korea in order to make another amphibious assault and cut off the retreat of the North Korean forces at Wonsan. There were long delays because of the many dangerous mines in the area. When Sergeant Harrison's unit came ashore early in the assault, they were surrounded by bodies and body parts washing in on the tide. To the north-west of Sergeant Harrison's position, the Seventh Marines engaged in a three- to four-day firefight, successfully defeating a Chinese division. They then started moving toward the Chinese border and the Yalu River. Sergeant Harrison was charged with guarding both the Korean and Chinese prisoners. November 10, 1950 marked the Marine Corps birthday, and it was at this time that the weather turned colder, and the Marines were issued winter weather gear at Wonsan, which included parkas and shoe packs.

On November 28 a group of US Marines, British Royal Marines, South Korean soldiers, US Army soldiers, and other civilian and military personnel were assembled in a task force commanded by Lieutenant Colonel Douglas B. Drysdale, commander of the Forty-First Royal Marine Commandos. His orders were to proceed from the village of Koto-ri to Hagaru-ri, approximately eleven miles to the north.

Snow lay deep on the hills on November 29, 1950, as the convoy moved along the road between Koto-ri and Hagaru-ri, heading toward the advance command post of the First Marine Division. At the head of the mixed column of men moved the tanks; behind them came a unit of British commandos in trucks, and behind the British came mail trucks carrying Christmas packages for the troops, chow trucks, ammo trucks, and a handful of Army infantry. The task force, nicknamed Task Force Drysdale, included liaison officers who served as couriers between the Marine regiments and division.

Huddled in the trucks, heads buried in their parka hoods against the cold, the men at first did not hear the sharp crack of small-arms fire from the Chinese. But when the mortars began to fall and the machine guns opened fire, the trucks skidded to a stop on the icy road, and the men dived for the ditch on the side of the road. It was not really a ditch, but a low place between the railroad embankment and the roadbed. The troops, including Sergeant Harrison, took cover there while the Chinese began to lob a steady rain of mortar shells into the ditch during the daylight hours. There had been some close air support from Marine Corsairs, but the Chinese were very well armed, and only the darkness saved them from total annihilation as the fire-fight continued into the night.[33]

Sergeant Harrison remembered that it was a clear, bright, starlit night, and the trucks that were burning on the road created more light. He could see the Chinese soldiers coming by the hundreds across the snow. They did not bother to creep or crawl, but just walked right up to the ditch, where the Marines continued firing. It was not a heavy firing, for in the bitter cold the M-1s and the carbines did not function well. The bolt would stop halfway back, and the Marine would have to put the butt of the weapon on the ground and kick the bolt back with his foot. Sergeant Harrison believed this was actually a good thing, because instead of using up ammunition recklessly firing in long bursts, they would pick a single Chinese and slowly

---

[33]   Harold H. Martin, "They Tried to Make Our Marines Love Stalin," *Saturday Evening Post*, vol. 224, no. 8, August 25, 1951.

and carefully fire, as if they were on the rifle range back in boot camp. A small dam went across one end of the ditch, which made a particularly good spot for shooting, as the Chinese would come down the bank from the road or the railroad and start up the ditch, two or three abreast. Sergeant Harrison and two other Marines, Morris L. Estess Jr. and Charles W. Dickerson, and an Army lieutenant, lay behind this little dam and let the Chinese keep coming until they were very close, and then shot them until they piled up in the ditch. But they still kept coming.[34]

In the ensuing engagement, Sergeant Harrison suffered a small wound on his left wrist from a rifle bullet and a splinter from a grenade between the knuckles of his right hand. The bullet did not bother him, he said, but the splinter hurt, so he started back down the ditch to where the wounded were being collected, and then he saw that the fight was hopeless. He knew that this situation was as bad as it had been at Wake Island, where the Japanese had captured him during the last war. Most of the men along the ditch bank were wounded, and their ammunition was almost gone. When he finally found a medic, there were seriously wounded men all around him, and Harrison felt ashamed to ask for treatment for such a small wound. So a Marine named James B. "Smokey" Nash took out his knife and pulled the splinter from Harrison's hand. Harrison returned to his position and resumed fighting, but at approximately 0300 on November 30, some type

---

[34] Ibid.

of high explosive projectile, probably a mortar shell, detonated about ten feet in front of his position, and he got the full blast of the concussion. No fragments struck him, but he started bleeding from the nose and mouth. When he regained consciousness almost an hour later, he was blind and deaf in one ear, his nose was broken, and his teeth were loosened. He staggered groggily when he tried to walk, so dazed and bleeding, Harrison crawled along the ditch, and up on the side of the railroad bank where he lay.[35]

When his head began to clear and the bleeding from his nose had stopped, he noticed that the stars were gone, and the sky was beginning to show the first glow of dawn. All the guns were silent, and soon Marine Major John McLaughlin came down the line of waiting men. Major McLaughlin was a well-decorated veteran who had fought at Guadalcanal, Cape Gloucester, and Peleliu in WWII. He informed the men that the Chinese had captured a GI and sent him back with the word that, if the trapped unit did not surrender in fifteen minutes, it would be wiped out. Major McLaughlin was taking a poll of the men to see what they wanted to do. If they said "Fight," he would fight. If they said to give up, then he would go back and tell the Chinese that, if they would give safe conduct to the wounded, the unit would surrender. There was some debate, for a few men wanted to hold out until daylight, when they believed the American planes would return, but the Chinese were so close that the planes could not strike

---

[35]   Ibid.

them without hitting the men in the ditch. To fight would have meant sure death to the wounded, for by now eight out of ten men were hurt and bleeding, or numb from concussion shock, and they were beginning to freeze.

With only about forty able-bodied defenders and almost no ammunition, Major McLaughlin reluctantly returned to the Chinese and agreed to surrender with the condition that his most serious wounded would be evacuated. A few minutes later, all along the railroad bank and across the narrow road and on the hills beyond, the Chinese stood up. They were on every side, some of them less than twenty feet away. Sergeant Harrison sat numb for a moment, and then he took the bolt from his carbine, threw it away, and began to walk unsteadily down the road. A Chinese soldier with a rifle ran toward him and grabbed Harrison by the hand, shaking it and slapping him on the back. But most of the Chinese were not paying much attention to the Americans. Instead, they were swarming over the unburned trucks, tearing open the Christmas packages and littering the ground with the bright paper as they tore into the boxes of cakes and cookies that families back in the States had sent to their soldiers.[36]

Soon, the approximately 143 men who were able to walk were assembled on the road in little groups, and the Chinese, fearing the planes would come back, marched them into the hills off the road where there were a few small houses. During their march, the prisoners saw a number of

---

[36]   Ibid.

dead and wounded Chinese soldiers. When they arrived at the houses and barns, the prisoners were crowded inside, and the Chinese brought them small servings of boiled potatoes. Once they had finished eating this meager meal, the Chinese searched them, patting their pockets for weapons, but leaving them their watches, rings, and fountain pens. They were then marched for another hour, deeper into the hills, to a hidden valley where there were some log huts in which they were allowed to sleep. To sleep, two men would lie close to each other for warmth, with one man's parka over their legs and the other parka over their upper bodies.[37]

The next morning they were fed again; breakfast consisted of a can of corn for each five men and a handful of boiled peas. They were then marched back down the mountain to the road where they had fought. Some of the wounded were still there, and they took blankets from the trucks and covered them and gave them cigarettes. They did not take the time to cover the dead who lay on the road and in the ditch where they had fallen, rigid with death and cold, and covered with torn pieces of bright Christmas paper that had been blown around the area by the wind.[38]

As the men passed the trucks, some snatched up bed rolls from where the Chinese had tossed them in the road, and stuffed their pockets with C rations. But most of the men were too numb and dazed to think clearly. Charles Harrison took a small notebook off a dead North Korean

---

[37]   Ibid.
[38]   Ibid.

body with the intention of writing down the names and addresses of all US prisoners he might meet so that a record of their presence would exist, whether they returned home alive or not. He hid a stubby pencil in his sock for this purpose.[39]

Handmade notebook carried by Charles Harrison to record the names of other POWs he met.

In single file, with Chinese guards beside them, they left the road and began to climb into the hills. For just short

---

[39]   Transcript.

of two weeks, they marched almost into Manchuria. The Chinese officers wore leather coats and fur caps, and they smoked lightly rolled cigarettes. The enlisted men, Snuffies, wore old blanket-type coats, and many wore sneakers. During the march, oxcarts were commandeered to carry the badly wounded. They would march by day when clouds protected them from planes, and when the days were clear, they would march by night. The men whose feet had been frostbitten during the battle in the ditch were the worst off, for the flesh began to break down into sores, and scabs would form on these sores during a long rest. When the men began to walk again, they would cry out as the scabs began to tear loose from the flesh. Occasionally, when hiding during the day, the men whose feet were causing them the greatest pain would get up to walk about, alarming the Chinese, who feared the planes would see a walking man. But the men would refuse to lie down, and the Chinese, though they threatened, never struck or punished them.[40]

The worst was the mountain climbs on icy trails at night. All the younger soldiers did their best to care for the older men, particularly one soldier named Gust Dunis, who was fifty-three years old. When he could go no further, he would suddenly sit in the middle of the trail, scooping up snow and rubbing it on his throbbing head, saying, "Shoot me, shoot me." Sergeant Harrison said of Gust Dunis, "He looked like some old patriarch out of the Bible, sitting in

---

[40]   Harold M. Martin, "They Tried to Make Our Marines Love Stalin," *Saturday Evening Post*, vol. 224, no. 8, August 25, 1951.

his sackcloth and pouring ashes on his head."[41] Their diet was boiled potatoes and hot water, for the Chinese were deathly afraid of the Korean water and would not drink it, nor let the prisoners drink it. When the potatoes ran out, they ate something that looked like sorghum seed and tasted like sand. The Chinese guards were eating no better than the prisoners.

When they slept in barns, the prisoners would sometimes find ears of dried corn, which they would steal and gnaw on during the march. They had to do this surreptitiously, for the Chinese had given strict orders against taking anything belonging to the people. In turn, the Chinese soldiers protected the prisoners from the people, for oftentimes, when passing through villages, North Koreans would try to strike, kick, or trip the tired men. The Chinese would drive the Koreans back with the butts of their guns. By this time, the men whose feet had been frozen began to die of gangrene. When they pleaded for medicine, the Chinese said they were sorry, but there was none to be had.[42]

Finally, sometime in late December 1950, the American POWs arrived at a camp near the small town of Kanggye, near the Yalu River, and about sixteen miles from the Manchurian border. The prisoners were divided up into squads and scattered throughout a one-hundred-acre area, billeted in Korean houses, farm shacks, and mud shacks. For the first few days, they were so tired and beaten that they did not move. They lay in the small houses and

---

[41]   Ibid.
[42]   Ibid.

would merely reach from beneath their parkas to take the food the Chinese put into their ration cans. Some men had no cans, and they ate the boiled sorghum seed, rice, bean curd, bean sprouts, and fish-head stew from their woolen caps, a very messy business.[43] After a few days in the camp, an outbreak of amebic dysentery effected many of the prisoners, some of whom did not survive the disease.

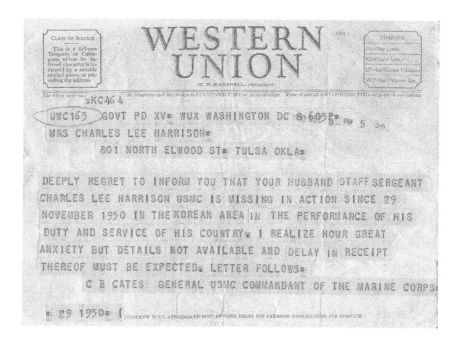

At about this time, Charles Harrison's wife, Mary, still living in Oklahoma, received a Western Union telegram from General C. B. Cates, commandant of the Marine Corps that read, "Deeply regret to inform you that your husband, Staff Sergeant Charles Lee Harrison USMC, is

---

[43]   Ibid.

missing in action since 29 November 1950 in the Korean area in the performance of his duty and service of his country. I realize your great anxiety but details not available and delay in receipt thereof must be expected."[44]

Major John McLaughlin was the senior Marine at the camp. He took on the difficult task of communication as the POWs were dispersed into many small groups in different locations. He established a chain of command and issued orders through five Marine SNCOs and NCOs, one of which was Sergeant Harrison. The Marines made every attempt to stick together. The guard force at the camp numbered over one hundred, in addition to thirty interpreters and administrative aides. The purpose of the aides was political, as it was their job to instruct and indoctrinate the POWs. Once the prisoners began to revive a bit, the Chinese began to interrogate them. At first, they did not ask many military questions, as they probably had gotten much information from the maps and papers the liaison officers were carrying when captured. Instead, they asked many personal questions, such as the following: How much money had the men earned as civilians? How much did their fathers make? Did they own an automobile? Did they own a house or land?[45]

A chubby Chinese female interrogator, bundled up in her quilted Chinese Army uniform, was very intrigued by the prisoner's private lives. At first, the men told the

---

[44] Interview with Jane Harrison Williams, 2015.

[45] Harold H. Martin, "They Tried to Make Our Marines Love Stalin," *Saturday Evening Post*, vol. 224, no. 8, August 25, 1951.

truth, but they often exaggerated, as they could see that she was enjoying it and imagining she could be a part of it. She asked Sergeant Harrison if he was wealthy enough to take his wife to a restaurant once a month, and he told her he could take her out four times a week if he felt like it.[46] Another prisoner, Smokey Nash, told her that he had a Cadillac and a Ford and a truck, and he and his wife and family went out to dinner at least three or four times a week and were never hurting for money for food or good clothing. Many of the POWs thought that this interrogator would have defected to enjoy a better life if she had ever been given an opportunity.[47]

Charles Harrison saw this entire propaganda campaign as almost comical. He speculated that the average Chinese soldier was likely a rice paddy coolie, fairly uneducated, and very susceptible to propaganda, and that the Chinese officers thought the average American service man came from the gutter and was likely on the same intellectual level.[48]

On occasion, the POWs and interrogators got into sharp arguments. One interrogator was an average-sized Chinese man named Pan, who spoke very good English. He claimed to be college educated, and believing that they would be more receptive to his rhetoric, he would pick out those prisoners who were staff NCOs or who had mentioned that they had a college degree and take them individually into another shack within the compound to inter-

---

[46]   Ibid.

[47]   Transcript.

[48]   Transcript.

rogate them about their private life. He would inform these prisoners that they were no longer slaves of American capitalists, as they had been "liberated" by the liberal Chinese People's Army. Sometimes, if he thought the prisoner was not absorbing this information properly, he would give the prisoner a written copy of his "speech" and insist that the prisoner copy it down in order to ensure that he remained awake. Harrison was told that the United States planned to invade China, and he laughed at that statement.[49]

Soon the POWs began to see that exaggerating their fortunes was the wrong tactic. As the questioning continued along the same lines, they began to revise downward their family income, the beauty of their family home, and the ease of their civilian life. They began to fabricate stories of their hungry childhood, a family income so small that there was no money left for clothing after buying food, of aged relations living on relief. This seemed to please the Chinese, and soon each man learned that when he was asked why he joined the Marines, it was best to say that he did it so he could be sure of food, clothing, and shelter, for he was afraid he would starve as a civilian.[50]

When the questioning finally took the turn the Chinese seemed to want, the true indoctrination began. During the day, the Chinese would gather the prisoners in a large barn-like structure with a straw roof and logs on which to sit, which they later called the Big House, and where the high

---

[49]   Harold H. Martin, "They Tried to Make Our Marines Love Stalin," *Saturday Evening Post*, vol. 224, no. 8, August 25, 1951.
[50]   Ibid.

commanders would proceed to rant and rave as they delivered their propaganda lectures. The POWs would huddle in the freezing barn and listen to these speeches that were sometimes three to four hours long, counting the pauses for translation from Chinese to English. These lectures would be on topics such as Wall Street warmongers and how the Americans were the aggressors.[51]

The prisoners learned to tell how long a man would speak by the way he was dressed. If he wore a fur cap with a leather bill, he wouldn't talk long. If he wore a fur cap with a leather bill and had a wristwatch and a fountain pen, he might speak an hour or two. If, however, he wore a fur cap with a leather bill, had a wristwatch, a fountain pen, and a leather jacket, and smoked tailor-made cigarettes, then he was an important person, and the POWs might have to huddle there in the cold for the better part of a day.[52] The weather was usually thirty to forty degrees below zero. The prisoners were required to sit on the cold floor or logs and would be punished if they attempted to stand up.

During the first meeting in the Big House, the speaker told them that they were not to think of or speak of themselves as prisoners. They were to think of themselves and refer to themselves as "newly liberated friends." The speaker said that the Chinese were not angry at them for being in Korea, for the Chinese realized it was not their fault. They had been duped by their aggressive, capitalistic,

---

[51] Transcript.
[52] Harold H. Martin, "They Tried to Make Our Marines Love Stalin," *Saturday Evening Post*, vol. 224, no. 8, August 25, 1951.

warmongering leaders and would therefore be treated with kindness. But if they disobeyed the rules, they would be severely punished. They would be made to stand at attention, or they would be rebuked in front of their fellows. To the Chinese, this was severe punishment. In after-action reports, the Marines said that the physical treatment by their Chinese captors was better than in most other POW camps. The Chinese seemed to adhere to this less violent policy, and as far as the Marines knew, they never struck, beat, or in any other way physically maltreated a prisoner.[53] However, many of the wounded and sick were told that they were being taken to the hospital, and most of them were never seen again.

At the end of a day of propaganda, the prisoners would return to their unheated shacks, where they slept on straw mats laid on mud floors and would huddle close together for warmth, trying to ignore the itching from lice. On sunny days, the Chinese would occasionally allow the prisoners to go into the yard outside the shacks and pick the lice off of themselves and each other. They were fed only twice a day, just enough for them to survive.

Three days after the first meeting in the Big House, the Chinese began their campaign to capture the men's minds. On Christmas Eve the Chinese decorated the Big House with wreaths, candles, two Christmas trees, red paper bells, and a sign that said, "Merry Christmas." They also hung the hall with huge placards that said, "If it were not for

---

[53]   Ibid.

the Wall Street Imperialists, you would be home with your wives and families on this Christmas night," and "Who is responsible for your being away from your wives and families at this Christmas time? We too want to be with our families." The speaker at this occasion wished the prisoners a Merry Christmas, denounced MacArthur, and "proved" that the Americans launched the war in Korea by showing a photograph of John Foster Dulles peering across the Thirty-Eighth Parallel toward North Korea. Some of the Americans had been forced to "volunteer" as speakers and got up to say that they had been forced by poverty into joining the military, and if it were not for this they would be spending Christmas at home with their families. At the end of the evening, the Chinese passed out gifts—ten tiny pieces of candy, six cigarettes, and a handful of peanuts.[54]

After Christmas, the lectures began in earnest. Lectures were held every other day, and on the days in between, the squads were supposed to hold group discussions at which the interpreters would take notes on what each man said. Copies of the *Shanghai News*, the *Peiping Daily News*, *People's China*, and the *China Review* were passed out and used as textbooks, and the men were to read the articles and comment on them. If a man did not have much to say, the interpreters, who were given nicknames by the POWs, such as Egg Head, BB Eyes, Stupe, the Snake, and

---

[54]   Harold H. Martin, "They Tried to Make Our Marines Love Stalin," *Saturday Evening Post*, vol. 224, no. 8, August 25, 1951.

Little Caesar, would take him aside and lecture him at great length, trying to clear his mind of "misconceptions."[55]

On one occasion, Staff Sergeant Harrison became quite ill with pneumonia. He knew that he was fairly close to dying when he was left alone in his shack and allowed to miss a mass propaganda session in the barn. Harrison was so ill that he could barely move and was going in and out of consciousness. The Chinese interrogator Pan seemed to sympathize with him and said he would try to get some medicine, which Harrison knew would never happen. He believed that the Korean farmers who owned the shack in which he was imprisoned were sympathetic to the POWs, and during one of his moments of consciousness, a hand, most likely belonging to one of the Korean farmers, came into his shack from underneath the straw wall and gave him a boiled egg and some white powder. He was terribly hungry, and he had never enjoyed an egg as much in his life. The next time water was available to him, he poured the white powder onto his tongue and drank it with the water, not knowing what the mixture actually was. Not long afterward, his condition began to improve.[56]

During the first week of January 1951, Sergeant Harrison was interrogated by Major Wei, CCF. He was questioned about his duties in the service, and he falsely stated that he was a duty NCO and that in Korea he was the labor NCO for his unit. Harrison later heard that all UN troops who were in any manner associated with the

---

[55]   Ibid.

[56]   Transcript.

intelligence service would not be released from captivity until the end of the war and that British soldiers would not be released. Later in January, Sergeant Harrison was interrogated by a CCF company grade officer and questioned about the financial status of himself and his family, his occupation as a civilian, his reason for entering the service, his length of time in the service, and where he had served.

Soon the word got around that the men who showed themselves to be the "most progressive" would be set free, and prisoners began to show great interest in the discussions. The men were also assigned to write themes on various subjects, which the interpreters would pore over for signs of progressiveness or political misconceptions. The best of these were printed in the camp newspaper, *The New Life*, and the lucky author was rewarded with two cigarettes and a personal note from the editor. The headlines over these essays were "Truman a Swindler," "I See the Light," and other similar titles. Sergeant Harrison found it fairly easy to write these little editorials and earn the reward. Late in the course of these lectures, which lasted for ten weeks, the Chinese decided to draw up a document similar to the Stockholm Peace Appeal, which all the "newly liberated friends" would sign. Sergeant Harrison was chosen to draft this document, which he did with great care, as he knew it would likely be broadcast in the United States. Unfortunately, Sergeant Harrison's draft diverged in some respects from the "truths" which had been taught by the Chinese, and Lieutenant Pan, the English-speaking interrogator, rewrote it. The men signed the draft prepared by

Lieutenant Pan, but the cold and malnutrition had cramped their hands, so some of the signatures were illegible, and others appeared to have been misspelled.[57]

As March of 1951 ended and the snow began to melt, the rumors got thicker that some of the most "promising friends" would be released. The prisoners were allowed to go outside in the sun, where they helped each other pick lice off their bodies. They were able to obtain a fifty-gallon steel drum in which to heat water, at least to body temperature, and take a bath. Eighteen men bathed in that water after not even being able to wash their hands all winter. By the time the last man was done, it no longer looked like water.

The prisoners were gathered together to begin a long trek south, along with their Chinese captors, by foot and by train. There was danger from the overhead planes, but the weather was warming up, and the men began to peel off their heavy winter gear and sometimes trade it for *yud*, a type of molasses candy. Their moods were improving, and one of the oldest Marines, Gust Dunis, would entertain the guards and the Koreans they passed by taking out his lower teeth and putting them back again, and he would charge them a handful of cigarettes for this diversion.[58]

During this trek, Staff Sergeant Harrison often tried to walk near his close friend, Master Sergeant Chester Mathis. One morning, they began a march over a high

---

[57] Harold H. Martin, "They Tried to Make Our Marines Love Stalin," *Saturday Evening Post*, vol. 224, no. 8, August 25, 1951.

[58] Ibid.

mountain in the rain. Everyone was weak from hunger, and when they reached the summit sometime after noon, the guards allowed them to rest. Sergeant Harrison and Master Sergeant Mathis dropped wearily onto a large flat rock. Looking out over the hills and valleys below, they saw a break appear in the rainclouds and a large rainbow arch across the sky. Mathis said, "You know, Harry, just over that rainbow is America and home."[59]

Somewhere south of Pyonggang, the prisoners were divided into two groups. Sixty of the more "progressive" men, which included Staff Sergeant Harrison, and twenty-three other Marines were separated from the rest. They were told by a guard they had nicknamed Stuttering Sam that they would be taken south to be released.[60] The remaining group, which included Marine Major McLaughlin and Master Sergeant Mathis, was marched to Chongsong and Pyokton, where they remained interned in POW camps for the duration of the war and where they suffered brutal and inhumane treatment.

The sixty prisoners in Staff Sergeant Harrison's group started walking south. After seven days, this group was split again into two groups of thirty, and these groups moved south by different routes. Sergeant Harrison's group was told that they were going to meet some "newly liberated friends" and they were to help the Chinese introduce them

---

[59]   Charles L. Harrison, "Twice across the Rainbow," USMC, *US Naval Institute Proceedings*, vol. 78, no. 5, May 1952.

[60]   Harold H. Martin, "They Tried to Make Our Marines Love Stalin," *Saturday Evening Post*, vol. 224, no. 8, August 25, 1951.

to their new life. They were to do this by explaining that the Chinese would not hurt them and would feed them as best they could. By this time, the food supply was very low, consisting primarily of a mush made from sorghum seed and sesame, which made their mouths raw. The Marines also helped the new prisoners fill out the questionnaires given them by their interrogators.

There was one question on military matters which the Marines would not let the new prisoners answer. This made the Chinese angry, and they called Staff Sergeant Harrison in and chewed him out, telling him that if they did not feel great sympathy for him for the years he had spent as a prisoner of the Japanese, they would punish him. Harrison twitched and jerked, as if his nerves were damaged, so the Chinese chose not to punish him.[61]

On May 18, 1951, eighteen Marines, including Staff Sargent Harrison, and one soldier, Corporal Saburo "Sam" Shimamura, the Army interpreter whom the Chinese thought was a Marine, were separated from the main group. This group was marched a few miles to the south to a river where they were given razors and soap and allowed to bathe and shave. They were fed well with rice and pork, which was the first time in six months they had seen anything other than sorghum seed or millet. The Chinese loaded up the Americans with books and leaflets on the peaceful aims of the Chinese, and they gave them surrender pamphlets, which they were told to pass out to their fighting com-

---

[61]   Ibid.

rades when they met them. "Success in your work," said the guard nicknamed Egg Head as he solemnly shook their hands.[62] The POWs were then moved south, passed from one group of guards to another, until they could hear the booming of the UN guns and could see the great beams of the searchlights lighting up the battlefield.

On the night of May 24, 1951, artillery shells whistled over the house in which the POWs and their captors were hiding and exploded against the hillside behind it. Their Chinese guards fled to the north in fear, and Staff Sargent Harrison firmly announced that he was not going north again. He was going home, and if anyone wanted to come with him, they were welcome. So all nineteen of the POWs sneaked off and waded across the shallow Imjin River. They ran for miles through the woods and, just before dawn, stopped in a field where the wheat was high and they could be hidden while they slept.

One of Charles Harrison's fellow Marines, Budd Caylor, gave an interview to *Reader's Digest* magazine in 1952, in which he related that the Marines awoke to find four Chinese soldiers pointing their guns at them. Harrison got up smiling, and using his limited Chinese, explained to the soldiers that they were released prisoners of war and the high command would be displeased if they were shot or taken back. The Chinese responded to Harrison, and in English, he quietly told the other POWs, "These birds aren't going to let us go. They're arguing whether they should

---

[62]   Ibid.

shoot us now or take us in." He continued to respond to the Chinese in a friendly manner, all the while giving his fellow POWs instructions: "Estess and Dickerson, get the one on the left. Caylor and Hilburn, the one on the right. Nash and Holcomb, the one next to him." Finally, Harrison gave the word "Let's get 'em," and the Marines did their jobs as assigned, leaving the bodies of the dead Chinese behind as they ran to a village where they were given shelter.[63]

Charles Harrison strongly denied that this event ever happened, saying, "At the time this *Reader's Digest* issue came out, I was on recruiting duty in Clinton, OK, and the radio and newspaper folks came down to the recruiting office. They had read this, and they were going to really make a big hero out of me, and I just had to put my foot down and say that it's strictly bull hockey."[64]

What did happen was that Staff Sergeant Harrison and Corporal Shimamura left in an attempt to find a friendly Korean who would take a message to the UN lines for them, and other prisoners stripped paper from the walls of the house and in an open field laid out a sign with the wallpaper strips saying, "POW HERE." From an old gun emplacement nearby, they were able to find shell casings which they used to spell out the word *"RESCUE"*. [65]

---

[63]　John G. Hubbell, "The Long Way Home," *Reader's Digest*, April 1952.

[64]　Transcript.

[65]　Harold H. Martin, "They Tried to Make Our Marines Love Stalin," *Saturday Evening Post*, vol. 224, no. 8, August 25, 1951.

When Harrison and Shimamura returned with an old Korean woman and her son who were willing to act as messengers, the other prisoners tried to discourage them because of the danger. The old woman insisted on helping them, saying to Staff Sergeant Harrison in Japanese that the Americans would not kill an old woman. She and her son were dispatched in opposite directions to make contact with the advancing United Nation tanks. In a few hours, both were back with notes. One note said, "Proceed toward the town of Chunchon and contact friendly troops there." The other note said, "Stay where you are. Friendly infantry will reach you soon."[66]

While they debated what they should do, a light plane with the markings A470, flew overhead, circled over their words in the field, and flew away. It returned with a message on a red streamer that read, "Come into the field to be counted. If any wounded, one man lie down across the panel."[67] They went into the field and stood in formation. Thirty minutes later came the roar of tank engines and three tanks of the Seventh Recon Company, Seventh US Division, came rumbling toward them. Charles Harrison remembered that the tanks looked beautiful, and even before the first tank—named Double Trouble—stopped, the GIs riding it jumped off with their hands full of C rations and cigarettes.[68] Before leaving the area, Staff Sergeant Harrison gave his parka to the North Korean farmer who owned the

66   Ibid.
67   Ibid.
68   Ibid.

house where they had taken refuge in the morning. The family of farmers waved as Corporal Shimamura, Staff Sergeant Harrison, and his fellow Marines rode the tanks back to Chunchon, feeling free for the first time since their capture.

At Chunchon, small observation aircraft flew them a few at a time back to Seventh Division CP, where they were deloused, dewormed, allowed to shower, and given Marine utility uniforms. At the naval hospital in Yokosuka, Japan, they spent several weeks having their medical needs met and being debriefed by General Van Fleet and intelligence officers. At this point, Staff Sergeant Harrison, who at 5 feet 9½ inches tall normally weighed 175 pounds, weighed about 115 pounds.

After being released from the hospital and returning to the states via Hawaii, Charles Harrison was finally on a train en route home to his wife and family. In his own words, Staff Sergeant Harrison reflected, "I believe that there and then I first began to grasp the full meaning of what had happened to me. Not so much in regard to my recent escape from the Chinese Communists in Korea, after being their prisoner for six months, but the fact that twice this wonderful freedom had been lost to me and both times miraculously restored… Now, speeding across the desert night… to Mary, my lovely Irish wife whom I had known and loved since childhood, to Pat, our four-year-old son, and to little Mike, whom I had never seen, a strange feeling of individuality took over. Why had the Great Skipper up there guided my course into those long years of oriental subjugation and both times brought me safely back into home port? Diagnosing my own feelings, now I knew that I was a better Marine, a better man, and by far a much better American than I would ever have been otherwise.

"No person who had ever known me well, especially Mary, would expect to find me bitter and disillusioned from my double dose of hard luck. I thought of many others, however, who as casual observers or acquaintances would probably expect to see a very dejected and spiritually broken Marine arrive home this second time. If only they could know how to appreciate America and 'things American' as I do!"

As the train ride continued, Charles Harrison finally slept. A jolt of the train awakened him just before dawn. He described this morning as "Slowly at first and then in marvelous splendor, God's paintbrush spread all the colors of the rainbow across the eastern sky... To me it was not only the start of a new day but of a new life. Almost six years before I had traveled this same route coming home from a much longer period of torture and confinement. I had lost and regained life and freedom twice, and now I was looking forward to a long leave with my family after which I could resume my Marine Corp career with an appreciation of life in my America that would be hard for the most eloquent speaker to describe."[69]

On a Saturday morning in June of 1951, Charles Harrison surprised his wife, arriving at the door of their

---

[69] Charles L. Harrison, "Twice across the Rainbow," USMC, *US Naval Institute Proceedings*, vol. 78, no. 5, May 1952.

home several hours before the family expected him. An embrace from Mary opened "the happiest day of my life" according to Harrison, a day in which he met his son Michael (who had been born on September 26, 1950, in Tulsa) for the first time and was reunited with four-year-old Patrick. Each time he picked up Michael, he murmured, "He's a dandy." While home for a thirty-day leave, Harrison reflected philosophically, "I don't much care to go back to the Orient. Every time I do, the people shoot at me and then lock me up. All I need now to make my education complete is a job by the Russians."[70]

After the joyful reunion with his family, Staff Sergeant Harrison was notified that he had been promoted to tech sergeant. Unbeknownst to Sergeant Harrison, a letter had been drafted by those who had accompanied him on his trek from the prison camp that eventually led to their freedom. In that letter was cited the leadership that Charles Harrison had exhibited, and a recommendation was made for his commissioning. Based upon the testimony in that letter, General Devereux recommended that Tech Sergeant Harrison be given a battlefield commission and made a second lieutenant. Charles Harrison was awarded the Purple Heart by Major General Robert E. Pepper for wounds sustained in action against the enemy on November 30, 1950. He was also awarded the Bronze Star Medal with Combat V for heroic achievement during operations against enemy aggressor forces on May 24 and 25, 1951.

---

[70]   Jim Harris, "Words Fail Tulsan, Once Red Prisoner, on Return," World Staff, *Tulsa Tribune*, Tulsa, OK, May 1951.

THE UNITED STATES OF AMERICA

TO ALL WHO SHALL SEE THESE PRESENTS, GREETING:
THIS IS TO CERTIFY THAT
THE PRESIDENT OF THE UNITED STATES OF AMERICA
HAS AWARDED THE

PURPLE HEART

ESTABLISHED BY GENERAL GEORGE WASHINGTON
AT NEWBURGH, NEW YORK, AUGUST 7, 1782
TO

First Lieutenant Charles E. Harrison, U.S. Marine Corps

FOR WOUNDS RECEIVED
IN ACTION

November 29, 1950, while a Staff Sergeant

GIVEN UNDER MY HAND IN THE CITY OF WASHINGTON
THIS   16th   DAY OF   June   1954

GENERAL, U.S. MARINE CORPS
COMMANDANT OF THE MARINE CORPS

James MacDonald wrote in an occasional paper in 1988 called "The Problems of US Marine Corps Prisoners of War in Korea," that "Sergeant Harrison had considerable experience with the Orientals. He had been captured by the Japanese at Wake Island on December 23, 1941, and held prisoner until his release on Hokkaido on 7 September, 1945. His previous experience as a prisoner of war taught him enough Japanese to gain information and to determine his general location from sign posts. He was helped in this regard by Corporal Saburo 'Sam' Shimamura, a US Army interpreter who had been attached to 1st Marine Division, and by Marine Corporal Andrew Aguirre, who learned how to speak Mandarin Chinese during a tour of duty in North China after World War II. Between them, they were able to converse with natives to keep informed of their location. As a matter of interest, Staff Sergeant Harrison compared the treatment by the Japanese and Chinese. As he put it 'The Japs hated our guts and were just plain mean. I admired them for this because they really believed in their cause and were loyal to it.' On the other hand, he refers to the false friendship and deceit of his Chinese captors."[71]

After a long vacation with his family, Second Lieutenant Harrison returned to active duty, attending recruiter school at Parris Island, South Carolina, followed by training at the area recruiter headquarters for the Southwestern US in Dallas, Texas. He was then assigned to Clinton, Oklahoma. The recruiting station was housed in the American Legion Building, where Harrison had his own office. His family was able to rent a small house in Clinton and enjoyed a year there together until his battlefield commission was made permanent and he was assigned to a Marine MP Company at Camp Elmore near Norfolk, VA. Charles and Mary welcomed their third son, Joe, on May 19, 1953.

On December 5, 1953, Second Lieutenant Harrison entered a request to be assigned to a course of instruction in Mandarin Chinese at the US Naval School, Naval Intelligence, US Naval Receiving Station in Washington, DC. Information he submitted with this request included:

A. Linguistic Background: Two (2) years High School Spanish.

---

[71] James MacDonald, "The Problems of US Marine Corps Prisoners of War in Korea," *Occasional Paper*, 1988.

B. Basic knowledge of Japanese and Mandarin Chinese; acquired from 3½ years as a Prisoner of War of the Japanese and 6 months as a Prisoner of War of the Chinese Communists.

C. Average grade in English: B.

His request was recommended for approval and forwarded by his commanding officers. Unfortunately for Harrison, despite his compelling application and unique qualifications for this assignment, on December 23, 1953, he received a notice from the commandant of the Marine Corps indicating that "the request… cannot be approved at the present time. The Marine Corps quota for attendance at the course in the subject school convening in January 1954 has already been filled."[72]

From Norfolk, Charles Harrison was assigned to the Fourth Marine Regiment as part of the First Provisional Air-Ground Brigade in Kaneohe, Hawaii. His battalion commander was John R. Lindsay, nicknamed Ironman Lindsay. He was a physical fitness enthusiast who had been an all-American collegiate wrestling champion in his weight class. He was short and all muscle, except for his head, as he was a very intelligent man. Lieutenant Harrison's introduction to Ironman Lindsay made it very clear that he was going to have to get into top physical shape if he was going to be a part of Lindsay's battalion.

Lieutenant Harrison was assigned as the executive officer (XO) of Alpha Company. The company com-

---

[72]   Military records courtesy of Beverly Harrison.

mander was Harold White, a chain cigar smoker, who was nicknamed Wizard. As his executive officer, Lieutenant Harrison learned much from Captain White, and when Captain White left the battalion, Colonel Lindsay made Harrison the company commander of Alpha Company, a duty he greatly enjoyed.

About six months later, when the commanding officer of Charlie Company retired, Harrison was made CO of Charlie Company, and shortly thereafter, Weapons Company.

While still in Hawaii, Harrison was called up to battalion staff as assistant S-3 to Major John Lauch. Charles and Mary had a nice home in Kaneohe Town, and on the weekends, when Charles was not out with the company on some training exercise, they would usually take their sons to Bellows or Kahuku for hikes and picnics. Charles and Mary enjoyed the beauty of Hawaii and had a number of picnics on the beach with their boys, using beach cottages and shacks that were sparsely furnished but livable for recreation. It was a beautiful location not only for training but for recreation.[73]

Charles Harrison suffered from back problems which may have been exacerbated by the treatment he received at the hands of his captors. Regardless of the cause, in 1956, at the age of thirty-five, Harrison underwent spinal disc surgery. In this same year, he received a promotion to captain. The following summer, in 1957, Captain Harrison

---

[73]   Transcript.

received orders to report to San Diego, where he became a company commander in the Third Recruit Training Battalion. After serving as company commander, he went to Recruit Training Command headquarters as a training inspector. His only daughter, Jane, was born in San Diego on December 26, 1957.

Complications from his back surgery, as well as an old ankle injury, prompted a doctor during an annual physical exam to send Harrison to Balboa Hospital in San Diego for further evaluation. Much to his displeasure, Captain Harrison was placed on temporary disability on June 30, 1960. His disability was considered to be "20% from complications of spinal disc surgery." While he was on temporary disability, Harrison held what he considered to be "petty civilian jobs," to supplement his disability pay, all the while making every effort to get back on active duty and keep in good physical condition. One of his civilian jobs was a laundry route from San Diego, which included parts of Camp Pendleton in Orange County, and it actually paid more than the Marine Corps. But in Charles Harrison's mind, it was "still civilian life," and he was very eager to get back to active duty. He wrote many letters to the Marine Corps in an attempt to return to active duty.[74]

Finally, in 1964, Charles Harrison was "found fit to perform" his duties, and he was removed from the Temporary Disability Retired List. He was recalled to active duty and reappointed in the US Marine Corps in the temporary

---

[74]   Ibid.

grade of major. Charles Harrison and his family, now consisting of three sons and one daughter, moved to Quantico, Virginia, where Harrison was assigned to the Amphibious Warfare School in Quantico. Harrison described this time as one of the toughest of his career, even tougher than two experiences as a POW. His second son, Michael, now a teenager, was using drugs, had run away from home multiple times and was having serious trouble at school on the base at Quantico. Harrison described his son as being "able to seek out the worst kids in any environment he happened to be in and join right in with them." Harrison felt as though his fellow Marines questioned his parenting abilities, which might also have led them to question his leadership capabilities. He felt that he did not do well in Amphibious Warfare School at Quantico because he had such a difficult time keeping his mind on it, while he worried incessantly about his son.[75]

After a tough nine months attending the Amphibious Warfare School in Quantico, Virginia, he completed the course on May 28, 1965. As the build up to the Vietnam War was occurring, Major Harrison was sent back to Headquarters Battalion, First Division at Camp Pendleton in California.

---

[75]   Ibid.

THE VIETNAM WAR

In 1965 Major Charles Harrison and his unit were sent to Okinawa, leaving his family in their quarters in Camp Pendleton. Major Harrison was assigned to Camp Courtney. Lieutenant Colonel William K. "Bill" Horn, an old friend of Harrison's, had been assigned as the commanding officer of Second Battalion, Third Marines, in Vietnam and had brought his battalion back to Okinawa. When Harrison learned that Horn had lost his executive officer, he telephoned him to let Lieutenant Colonel Horn know that he would very much like to be assigned to him as his next XO. Bill Horn was able to use his influence to arrange this transfer, and Harrison served as his executive officer from December 24, 1965, until July 15, 1966, when Lieutenant Colonel Horn was detached.

Upon his arrival, Major Harrison was successful in getting his outfit a number of quotas at the Jungle Warfare School, which the Marines called Andersonville, near Subic Bay in the Philippines. The Little Negritos really challenged them during their jungle warfare training. Major Harrison's battalion was filled with many Vietnam veterans on their second tour of duty. They were in good shape, and most of them were combat-hardened Marines, good staff NCOs, and good officers, of which Major Harrison was very proud. After completing training in the Philippines, the battalion boarded the USS *Valley Forge* and made company-sized raids up and down the coast of Vietnam for a few months.

His battalion went on their first major operation, which was called Operation Double Eagle, in Quang Ngai Province. In a statement of commendation, Lieutenant Colonel Horn stated, "During the planning phase for Operation Double Eagle, Major Harrison was able, by dint of long hours and hard work, to coordinate all planning in such a manner that the operation was virtually flawless. He overlooked no details and it is to his credit that both the amphibious landing and the operation itself progressed on perfect schedule."[76]

They landed the battalion by helicopter on an old French airfield about twenty miles inland, right on the bank of the Song Tu Bong River. Tactics dictated that the battalion be split into two segments. Major Harrison assumed command of Command Group Bravo, and with two rifle companies, he operated independently for the remainder of the operation. Lieutenant Colonel William Horn took the other segment of the battalion on a foot patrol operation, and they were gone for several days. On the first day

---

[76] Statement of Lt. Col. W. K. Horn, USMC, commanding officer, Second Battalion, Third Marines, from November 4, 1965, to July 15, 1966.

they were gone, Major Harrison's companies took fire from across the river. He realized too late that they were in a bad position because they were wide open to enemy fire, and the enemy were likely inside tunnels. The units would need to cross the river, which was very deep at that point, to get to them. They were too close for artillery fire, but they did open up with mortar fire. His units were able to get some assistance from helicopter gunships, but they continued to take some very accurate rifle fire. Major Harrison lost several people from his companies, and one helicopter took a shot in the oil pan while trying to evacuate the wounded and had to make an emergency landing just out of range of the rifle fire. A second helicopter flew in with the necessary parts and a mechanic to fix the problem. One crew member was killed during the landing when that second helicopter was also disabled. The Marines could not see any muzzle flashes, so they were firing blindly at the enemy in an exchange that did not last more than thirty minutes.

Major Harrison remained in radio contact with Lieutenant Colonel Horn and his units, who were about twenty miles away. Lieutenant Colonel Horn's units were not sure they were on course when they started back toward the battalion position. In the middle of the night, Bill Horn called for illumination from Major Harrison's position, so Harrison roused up the eighty-one Mortar crew to fire illumination rounds into the air, and Lieutenant Colonel Horn and his men were able to return to their perimeter on the riverbank early the next morning.

Ultimately, the Navy cruiser USS *Helena* provided accurate gunfire from eight-inch rounds whistling overhead. Major Harrison's spotters up on the line reported back that the gunfire was right on target. Of this event, Lieutenant Colonel Horn wrote that Charles Harrison, "Displayed exceptional qualifications for field command in combat by aggressively and adeptly leading the Bravo element while it was in direct contact with Viet Cong forces."[77]

The entire battalion was able to get back to Valley Forge. From there, the unit was taken by helicopter back to Third Division Headquarters on Hill 327 and took up a position on the back side of the hill. They worked out of that area for some time and were attacked a number of times, usually at night. They had a fairly strong perimeter and had had time to put up barbed wire as they brought the battalion up to strength. They worked company-sized patrols out of that camp before the entire battalion moved to the small village of Dai Loc, which was about twenty miles inland from Da Nang. There they set up an operating base in a heavily mined old French fort. The men had to carefully watch their step as they tried to avoid the mines. Engineers came in to remove the mines, but they did lose several people before they could all be removed.

The remainder of Major Harrison's tour was spent patrolling out of Dai Loc, where the battalion headquarters remained in that old French fort. His battalion position did take some light casualties during night raids, but the

---

[77]   Ibid.

Vietcong casualties were much heavier. After one particular raid in the middle of the night, with heavy fire from both sides, the Vietcong were fought off. In the morning, Major Harrison went outside to look over the casualties and found that there were quite a few dead Vietcong bodies. One VC lying on his face looked somewhat familiar, so Major Harrison used his foot to turn the body over. He recognized the body as belonging to a native Vietnamese whom they had recently allowed to come into their camp as a barber. This was seen as a lesson to all the Marines to be very careful who they allow into their perimeter, as they could be taking important information out with them when they leave.

In September of 1966, Major Harrison returned to base headquarters of the Twenty-Fifth Marines at Camp Pendleton. Harrison remained there for almost a year, all the while desiring to get back into an infantry unit. When he heard that the Second Battalion, Twenty-Eight Marines, was re-forming at Camp Pendleton and that the commanding officer was a chunky bespectacled fireplug of a Marine named Walter "MuMu" Moore, he saw his chance. Lieutenant Colonel Moore was a good friend of one of Harrison's best friends, Bob Maden; therefore, Harrison contacted Bob Maden and told him, "Hey, Colonel Moore is a friend of yours. Tell him that old Charlie Harrison is sitting idle at base headquarters, itching to get back into things."[78] Lieutenant Colonel Moore did get Major

---

[78]   Transcript.

Harrison transferred and made him the commanding officer of the Second Battalion, Twenty-Eighth Marines, in July of 1967.

The battalion was made up primarily of Vietnam veterans, some of them getting ready to go back for their third tour of duty. The battalion underwent a number of training exercises. On one occasion, they did a landing exercise at Pendleton, and Major Harrison was acting as CO of troops. He was sent to board the ship, and it turned out to be the APA *George Clymer*, the very ship he had been aboard as a platoon sergeant when he made the landing at Inchon. Major Harrison was welcomed aboard by the commanding officer of the *George Clymer* and thought to himself, "My God, last time I was aboard this old ship, everybody had diarrhea, they were starving to death, and glad to make landing anywhere. Inchon was welcome."[79]

In July of 1967, Major Harrison was working late one night, and Bob Sheridan, who had been in the same battalion with Harrison in Vietnam and was now working in Washington, DC, called Harrison. He said to Harrison, "You know, your battalion is probably going to go right back into Vietnam. You have almost thirty years in now. You've already been over there for one tour, and if you take that battalion back, you're probably going to get your butt shot off. Therefore, I'm going to transfer you, and you tell me where you'd like to go." Harrison's reply was, "Oh, Bob, I'd rather take my chances and stay with the battalion."

---

[79]   Transcript.

Sheridan was not going to accept that answer. He said, "No, now Fallbrook is open, Marine Barracks Fallbrook." A few days later, Charles Harrison was sent orders to report to the Marine barracks at the Naval Ammunition Depot (NAD) in Fallbrook, California, as commanding officer, which would be his final tour of duty in the Marine Corps.[80]

Duty in Fallbrook was very pleasant. Most of the Marines were Vietnam veterans, very dependable and hard-working, which made Major Harrison's job easy. The family had beautiful quarters in Fallbrook, living in a Spanish-style home with a red-tile roof and an enclosed courtyard, and they made many close friends on base.

The NAD in Fallbrook was a small base adjacent to Camp Pendleton in a very rural setting. There were many small animals, such as coyotes and rabbits, roaming the base. At one point, the US government sent a trapper to the base in an attempt to control the wild population.

The trapper set hundreds of heavy steel jaw traps throughout the base. Many people consider these types of traps to be cruel and inhumane, and Charles Harrison was one of those people. Once the trapper left the base, Charles Harrison and his young daughter, Jane, would head out in the dark each night, after Harrison's work day was over, carrying sticks, bats, or fishing poles—anything that they could use to spring the traps. Charles Harrison understood imprisonment and suffering, and he did not want even the

---

[80]   Transcript.

coyotes or rabbits to experience this cruel treatment. He valued all life, no matter how small.

The result of this clandestine action on the part of Charles and Jane was that critters continued to roam the Fallbrook base. Eventually, Jane was given a puppy that resulted from the mating of a coyote and a German shepherd.[81]

In 1968 Major Harrison was promoted to Lieutenant Colonel. On June 30, 1969, at the age of forty-eight, Lieutenant Colonel Charles Harrison was honorably discharged from the United States Marine Corps.

---

[81] Interview with Jane Harrison Williams.

CIVILIAN LIFE

Charles and Mary pondered where they would like to live in retirement. Charles had a cousin who was a doctor in Auburn, California, and he spoke highly of nearby Grass Valley. Charles thought that some exploration of Northern California was in order. He took a ten-day leave, and he and his old dog, Daisy, took off on a camping trip. He drove up toward the Oregon border and then started heading south, camping along the way and checking out different communities. When he arrived in Grass Valley, he thought that it seemed ideal because it was close to Beale Air Force Base, which would provide a commissary and medical care, and Sacramento was only sixty miles in one direction, with Reno about eighty miles in the other direction. After returning to his family in Fallbrook, Harrison brought Mary and his children to Grass Valley to look it over, and they all liked it very much.

The family decided to move to a two-and-a-half-acre property high on a hill in the Peardale area of Grass Valley. At the time of the move, their eldest son, Patrick, was attending Northern Arizona University, pursuing a degree in forestry. Michael was living in the California Bay Area, and Joe and Jane were attending school at Camp Pendleton.

Once they settled into their new home, Joe enrolled at Nevada Union High School, and Jane was placed in sixth grade at Lyman Gilmore Elementary School. One and a half acres of their new property was mostly devoted to apple trees, which kept Charles very busy. He and Mary easily became involved in their new community. After meeting the police chief, Mel Mauser, he became an auxiliary police volunteer, and Chief Mauser allowed Charles to begin a project microfilming police records. Charles participated in some stakeouts and was often able to ride with the regular patrols around Grass Valley. He enjoyed the men and women who worked with the department, and he liked the discipline, which reminded him of his time with the Marine Corps.

Charles and Mary Harrison had become active in the Grass Valley Historical Society, and through this connection, they met a retired Army colonel, Chuck Graydon. Colonel Graydon had a long military record. He had been in the Army cavalry back when they still rode across the prairies on their favorite horse with the flag whipping in the wind. He had ridden in tanks in World War II, but like Charles, Chuck Graydon was currently interested in the local Immigrant Trail and wanted to write a book about it. Charles Harrison had a good camera, an Argus C-5, and offered to take photographs for the book. Most of the photographs used in that book, which was published and entitled *First Wagons over the Sierra*, were taken by

Charles Harrison. Charles and Chuck often went camping together in the mountains and desert, taking their dogs, an enormous mongrel, and a small dog called Buckwheat, with them. They remained very close friends until Chuck Graydon's death, approximately one year after their book was published.[82]

For some time, Charles drove the Nevada County Bookmobile, bringing reading material directly to the reader. During slow times during his days on the Bookmobile, he would read some of the books he was transporting. He was very open to new ideas and became interested in reading about life after death and near-death experiences, perhaps reflecting on the number of times he found himself on the precipice of losing his own life.[83] He also loved history, and in addition to providing photographs for Chuck Graydon's book, he wrote a number of magazine articles on various topics.

Charles Harrison was an accomplished furniture maker, crafting beautiful pieces from fine, heavy wood. He built chests, tables, benches, and a beautiful desk and chair for his young daughter. Much of his work incorporated heart-shaped cut outs into the wood, which his daughter viewed as a sweet and sensitive theme for a very tough and resilient man. He also learned to play the organ, entirely by ear. He never could read a note of music, but played well enough to thoroughly entertain his family and friends. Besides his love of camping and hiking, Charles and Mary

---

82   Transcript.
83   Interview with Jane Harrison Williams, 2015.

both took up cross-country skiing, as they were living so close to the Tahoe area slopes.[84]

In June of 1992, at the age of seventy-one, Charles Harrison was reunited with his old friend and fellow POW, Saburo "Sam" Shimamura. At that time, Sam Shimamura was living in Salt Lake City, Utah, with his wife, Katie. The reunion took place in Grass Valley, at which time the two friends credited each other with helping one another get through the extremely adverse circumstances they shared. They recalled that during the long marches, they often spent the night in old barns or shacks. The farmers that had previously used the barns had kept strings of peppers suspended in batches from the ceiling. Shimamura said, "We put the peppers in our pockets in an attempt to keep our hands warm." They also remembered finding old moldy tobacco in the abandoned structures and said that smoking that tobacco together brought a small bit of comfort to the group.

Charles Harrison summed up the reunion of the two by saying, "I couldn't ask for a finer friend than Sam. His support helped me get through the worst of times. I'm forever grateful to this forever friend."[85]

Charles and Mary Harrison welcomed two grandchildren, Matthew and Amanda, before Mary's death on October 22, 1999, at the age of seventy-five. On November 21, 2007, Charles married Beverly Baker in Grass Valley,

---

[84]   Interview with Jane Harrison Williams, 2015.

[85]   Jane Harrison Wilson (now Williams), "Korean War Buddies Have Reunion," in *The Union*, Grass Valley, CA, June 19, 1992.

and they remained married until Charles's death. On August 11, 2011, he received the unfortunate diagnosis of Dementia. Almost four years later, on Saturday, January 17, 2015, at the age of ninety-three, Charles Lee Harrison passed away in his Nevada County home. In addition to his widow, Beverly, he was survived by three children, Patrick, Joe, and Jane, his two grandchildren, and two of his sisters, Ruth and Peggy.

As General James L. Jones, then the commandant of the Marine Corps, stated in his letter to Charles Harrison on December 13, 2001, "Your record of valor and combat extends to circumstances far greater than most have had to endure. The tremendous courage with which you faced more than four years of captivity by the enemy in two separate conflicts is nothing short of extraordinary. Under such conditions, other men might have given up hope, but you did not. Your story of unfailing bravery against insurmountable odds is an inspiration to us all, and although there are many who will never know the tremendous sacrifices you've made in defense of the nation's freedom, the nation is forever in your debt. As you well know, our ties to the Corps and our sense of duty don't end when we hang up the uniform. Although many years have passed since you left our active ranks, your love for the Corps and your fellow Marines has been a constant in your life. Your continuing devotion to your brothers in arms is the embodiment of our cherished motto, Semper Fidelis."[86]

---

[86] Letter to Charles Harrison from General James L. Jones, commandant, USMC, December 13, 2001.

Charles Harrison was an inspiration to all who knew him, both in military and civilian life. Although he has the unique position of having been a prisoner of war in two different wars, he was an extraordinarily humble man who deeply loved his country and the Marine Corps and believed that "there are no personal heroics or anything out of the ordinary about my career. I was just an everyday Marine. I hopefully did my job, and did it well… but there are thousands and thousands of Marines out there with more impressive careers and backgrounds than mine… I consider myself one of the most fortunate men in the world to even be alive, to start with, and to any hardship or tough times that I've experienced in my 30 years in the Corps, I dedicate them to the memory of the Marines who didn't come back."[87]

Charles Harrison was much more than "just an everyday Marine" who did his job well. He was a Marine who deserves to be remembered and acknowledged for his extraordinary service and sacrifices. His character and his philosophy of life can best be summed up in his own words: "Life is very good, twenty-four hours each day, for the person who wishes to make it so. Some of us must bear a few more hardships than others, but in each of these hardships there is a humble lesson to be learned by him who will accept it as such." [88]

Semper Fidelis.

---

[87] Transcript.

[88] Charles L. Harrison, "Twice across the Rainbow," USMC, *US Navy Institute Proceedings*, vol. 78, no. 5, May 1952.

MEDALS AND COMMENDATIONS

American Campaign Medal
American Defense Service Medal
Armed Forces Reserve Medal
Asiatic-Pacific Campaign Medal with one star
Bronze Star Medal with Combat V
China Service Medal
Combat Action Ribbon
European-African Campaign Medal
Good Conduct Medal with three stars
Korean Presidential Unit Citation
Korean Service Medal with two stars
Marine Corps Expedition Medal with Silver W
Marine Corps Reserve Ribbon
Navy Commendation Medal with Combat Distinguishing
    Device
Navy Occupation Service Medal
Navy Presidential Unit with two stars
National Defense Service Medal with one star
Organized Reserve Medal
Presidential Unit Citations with four stars

Prisoner of War Medal (Korea)
Prisoner of War Medal (WWII)
Purple Heart Medal
United Nations Service Medal
Victory Medal World War II
Vietnam Campaign Medal with device
Vietnam Service Medal with three stars
World War II Victory Medal

BIBLIOGRAPHY

This book is based upon transcripts of over ten hours of recorded interviews with Charles L. Harrison by General Orlo K. Steele (USMC, retired), which took place in Grass Valley, California, in 2002 (referred to as "transcript").

Additional oral history courtesy of Jane Harrison Williams, interviewed by the authors for this book in 2015.

Archdiocese for the Military Services, USA: Washington, DC, Sacramental Certificates (1946/1947).

Daugherty, Leo J., III. *Train Wrecks and Ghost Killers: Allied Marines in the Korean War.* Marines in the Korean War Commemorative Series.

Dobbins, Mike. "Wars Last a Lifetime—for the Living as well as the Dead," in *The Union* (Grass Valley, CA), vol. 121, no. 179, May 28, 1986.

Cressman, Robert J. *A Magnificent Fight: Marines in the Battle for Wake Island.*

Estess, Morris L., Jr. *One US Marine's Version of Task Force Drysdale, Hell Fire Valley, and POW Status in Korea 1950–52.*

Harris, Jim. "Words Fail Tulsan, Once Red Prisoner, on Return," in *Tulsa Tribune* (Tulsa, Oklahoma), May 1951.

Harrison, Charles L. Letter dated April 12, 1944.

Harrison, Charles L. "Twice Across the Rainbow," in *US Naval Institute Proceedings*, vol. 78, no. 5, May 1952.

Harrison, Don M. *A Brief History of Harrison Memorial United Methodist Church*, 1948.

Hubbell, John G. "The Long Way Home," in *Reader's Digest*, April 1952.

"Invasion, The," in *Life Magazine*, vol. 29, no. 4, October 2, 1950.

Keene, R. R. "The Japanese Strike in the Pacific," in *Leatherneck* (magazine of the Marines), December 1991.

"'Let's Get 'Em,' Tulsan Said, and 19 Escaped from Reds," staff story published in the *Tulsa Tribune* (Tulsa, Oklahoma), 1952.

Martin, Harold H. "They Tried to Make Our Marines Love Stalin," in *Saturday Evening Post*, August 5, 1951.

Melson, Charles D. *Condition Red: Marine Defense Battalions in WWII*, 1966.

Nelson, Mary Jo. "They Defended Wake Island," in *Sunday Oklahoman*, December 19, 1982.

O'Brien, Cyril J. "Wake's Defenders," in *VRW Magazine*, January 1980.

Poindexter, Arthur A. "Wake Island: America's First Victory," in *Leatherneck* (magazine of the Marines), December 1991.

Renda, Matthew. "A Veteran Recalls a Holiday on the Brink," in *The Union*, vol. 147, no. 50, December. 23, 2011.

Simmons, Edwin H. *Frozen Chosin: US Marines at the Chang Jin Reservoir*, in Korean War Commemorative Series, 2002.

Urwin, Gregory J. W. *Facing Fearful Odds: The Siege of Wake Island*, 1997.

Williams, Jane Harrison Wilson. "Korean War Buddies Have a Reunion," in *The Union*, June 19, 1992.

Wukovits, John. *The Battle for Wake Island*, 2003.

ABOUT THE AUTHOR

Leo LaBrie was born in New Bedford, Massachusetts, the home of *Moby-Dick*, in 1934 to Florida LaBrie and Aime LaBrie. Leo was one of six children. He attended St. Hyacinth School, New Bedford High, and El Camino College. He enlisted in the Air Force in 1951 and was honorably discharged in 1955. He moved to California and worked as an engineer for two mobile home manufacturers. He worked for Northrop Aircraft as an assembler, and following his schooling as a draftsman, he worked for Autonetics Aircraft and Douglas Aircraft as a drafting engineer.

He married Gail Bolton in 1965 and raised two daughters, Laura and Carol. Gail passed away in 2007 from cancer. Leo is a forty-year member of the Elks Lodge and thirty years in the Knights of Columbus. Leo is active in St. Patrick's Catholic Church and attends Mass daily, weather permitting. He no longer drives but uses a cane and commutes with a battery-operated scooter provided by the Veterans Administration. He enjoys working on his computer. He was editor of three club bulletins when you had to cut and paste. Today he does everything on the computer. He thanks the good Lord that he can still continue what he enjoys doing at his age.

Theresa McLaughlin was born and raised in San Diego, CA, where she graduated from San Diego State University with a degree in English Literature. She served as an administrative assistant in several law offices, a private school, and the non-profit sector in Southern California, before moving to Novato, CA with her husband and two children in 1986. While raising her children, Theresa enjoyed a 17-year career with a group travel company, where her responsibilities included both marketing and operations.

Now living in Nevada City, CA with her husband, Theresa McLaughlin works as a volunteer for several non-profit organizations and is a regular columnist in her local newspaper, *The Union*.

CPSIA information can be obtained
at www.ICGtesting.com
Printed in the USA
FSHW012306080320
67846FS

9 781684 092116